FIGURES IN A
LANDSCAPE

FIGURES IN A LANDSCAPE

A Guide to the great historical characters of North Wales

Part One:

The first thousand years

MICHAEL SENIOR

'Let us now praise famous men . . . ' – Ecclesiasticus. 44.i.

GWASG Carreg Gwalch

ISBN: 0-86381-469-7

Cover design: Smala

*First published in 1997 by Gwasg Carreg Gwalch,
12 Iard yr Orsaf, Llanrwst, Conwy, Wales, LL26 0EH.
☎ (01492) 642031*

Printed and Published in Wales.

Contents

PART TWO (To follow)
Madocks
The First Marquess of Anglesey
Lloyd George
Sir Clough Williams-Ellis

Author's Preface

To date in my books and local booklets about North Wales I have been mostly concerned with the land itself. Here I turn to the people within it. Doing so, I should say a word or two about the principles by which they are chosen.

In the history of North Wales a few figures stand out not just in local but in any terms. They tower over the land like indestructible peaks formed out of granite. Those I deal with here all have that quality. You cannot mistake them for being anything other than giants.

The other defining quality I have looked for is that of being linked by birth or residence with North Wales. Not all the people in this book were born here. Lloyd George himself, for instance, was born in Manchester. So close is his connection with North Wales that even though his impact was on Great Britain as a whole he remains in our eyes, as he was in his own, a man of North Wales. The first Marquess of Anglesey was born in London, and his family had their other seat in Staffordshire, but though the field of his success was notably elsewhere, he identified himself so closely with North Wales that it was from his property here that he took his greater title.

So much for the general principles behind the selection of these figures. They are to a large extent self-selecting. The facts of history throw up a slight anomaly, and the modern reader will perhaps note that this book is not politically correct. It does not practise positive discrimination. To be blunt, there are no women in it. This is not by choice but as a result of those facts. It is due to no chauvinistic attitude, but is in fact a sad reflection on the opportunities available to women in North Wales' past. It is not my fault if history has hitherto been hard on women. Let us be thankful that they are now making up for it.

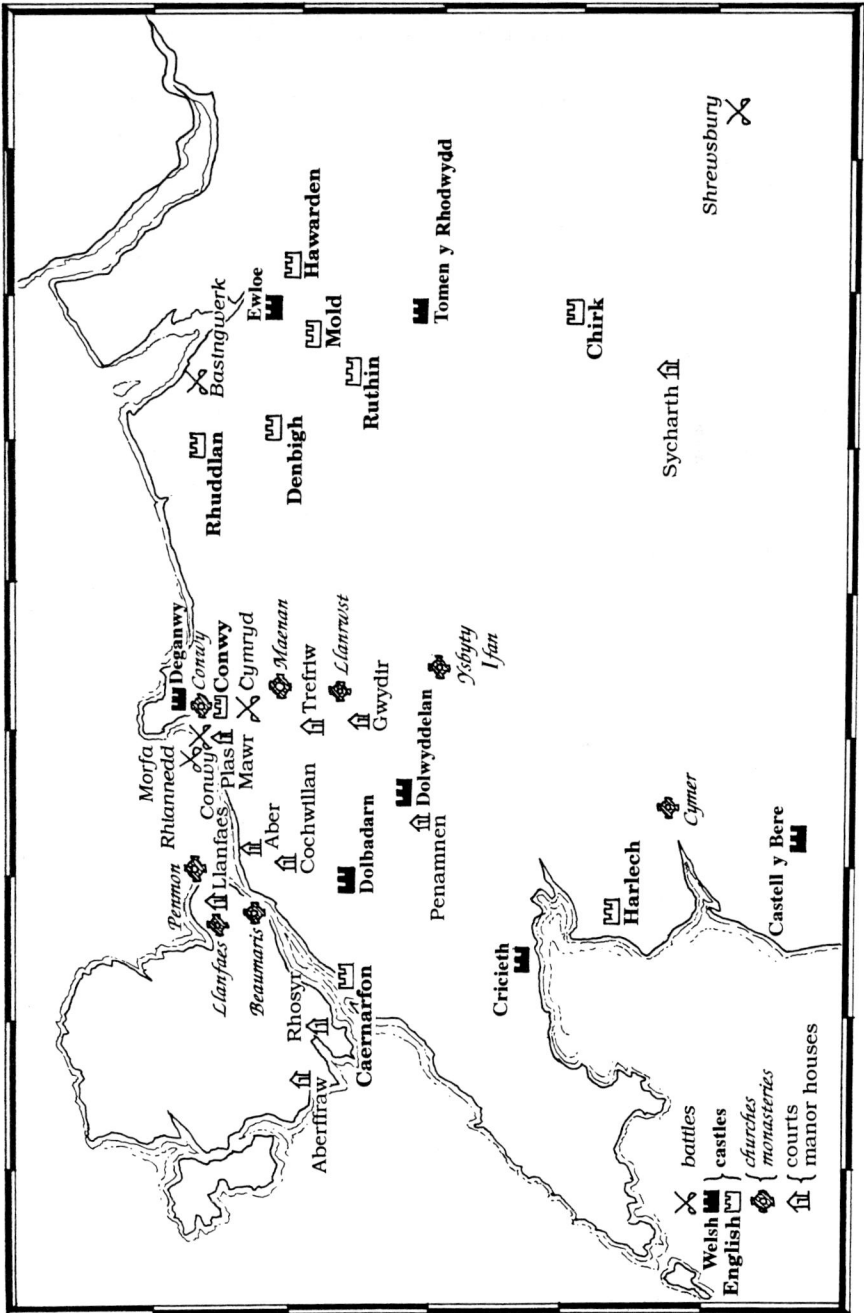

Shrewsbury ✗

Hawarden ▥
Ewloe ▥
Mold ▥
Tomen y Rhodwydd ▥
Chirk ▣
Bastngwerk ✗
Ruthin ▥
Denbigh ▣
Rhuddlan ▥
Sycharth ⌂

Deganwy ▥
Conwy ⚙
Conwy ▣
Cymryd ✗
Maenan ⚙
Trefriw ⌂
Llanrwst ⌂
Gwydir ⚙
Ysbyty Ifan ⚙
Morfa Rhianedd
Conwy ✗
Llanfaes Plas Mawr ⌂
Aber ⌂
Cochwillan ⌂
Dolwyddelan ▥
Penmon ⚙
Llanfaes ⌂
Beaumaris ⚙
Dolbadarn ▥
Penamnen
Cymer ⚙
Rhosyr ⌂
Caernarfon ▥
Harlech ▥
Cricieth ▥
Castell y Bere ▥
Aberffraw ⌂

✗ battles
▥ } castles
⚙ { churches / monasteries
⌂ { courts / manor houses

Welsh ✗ ▥
English ▣

Maelgwn

The Vardre above Deganwy is said by some to be a volcanic plug, and perhaps around it you can see the broad rim of a crater. To the less prosaic it cries out to have a fairytale castle on top of it, and you do not have to be particularly romantic to see this as a prime romantic setting.

For the same reason, of course, it has been prominent in history as well as in the landscape. In fact its historical role imposes itself on the area's history as strikingly as its physical form intrudes into the view.

If the history of North Wales has bedrock, this is it. Its struggle, its independence, and indeed its ultimate disintegration originated here, where Maelgwn founded the house of Gwynedd.

Indeed the figure of that distant king casts a long shadow forward, bearing as he does a double nature, and so a double influence: one type of influence over our factual and political development, and another over the traditions and the background culture of the nation. Because the two are so different we can easily distinguish the facts from the fantasy. First, then, the facts.

When the Romans left the island of Britain they left much of it in disorder. The natives, accustomed to being governed and controlled by that massive military might, had become unused to organising themselves, and in this western corner, with which we are concerned, they found themselves drastically overrun by invading tribes from across the Irish Sea. Eventually it was found necessary to send for help, and a group of more militant and better-organised compatriots came south from the area of the Roman wall to rid North Wales of the Irish invaders. In about 400 A.D. they formed a base here under their leader Cunedda, and it is from him that the ancestry of Maelgwn and the house of Gwynedd, and hence of the royal line of Wales, may be traced.

Since they were concerned with protecting the coast from raiders from the west, this Deganwy hilltop with its excellent seaward views would have been a suitable base for them, and there is archeological evidence too for the occupation of this natural citadel at this time. Tradition has

The hill above Deganwy known as the Vardre is an early defended site.

always located Cunedda here, and so we may reasonably suppose that when King Maelgwn, the most prominent of Britain's 'dark age' kings, reigned, as he almost certainly did, at Deganwy in the mid 6th century, he was occupying the seat of his ancestors founded about a century and a half before his time.

Maelgwn was the great-grandson of Cunedda. Since it took some time, perhaps more than one generation, to drive the Irish out of North Wales, he was probably the first person to be in a position to establish Gwynedd as a stable kingdom. Before the Romans came the Venedotae (from whom the kingdom takes its name) had been one tribe among several occupying North Wales, and during Roman times when the concept of kingdom occurred (as in the case of Cartimandua, or during the revolt of Caractacus) it was either put to use or suppressed, according to which was the politically wise move at the time. Now, temporarily freed from both sets of invaders, a real and meaningful kingdom could rise into prominence in this corner of North Wales.

It is mainly from archeology that we know that this is what took place. The Welsh Annals tell us only one thing about Maelgwn, and that is his death: he died in 547, the year of a great epidemic. Given this date, and tradition's location of the king at Deganwy, we may legitimately suppose that the sixth century finds there relate to him, in much the same way as we relate the gold of Mycenae to Agamemnon. Archeology tells us of a stable and luxurious court here during the sixth century, one which (from the evidence of a dozen or so pieces of amphorae) was able to import wine from the eastern Mediterranean.

This evidence for Maelgwn's factual prominence may seem slight, and it would indeed be insufficient if it were not supported by other material. Perhaps indeed Maelgwn would be relegated to the category of folktale, if it were not for Gildas.

N.J. Higham, in his book *The English Conquest*, quite rightly warns us not to try to read Gildas as history. His work was polemical, and had the overriding purpose of trying to persuade his contemporaries to restore their good relations with God, the failure of which has brought on them the curse of the Saxon invasion and revolt. Nevertheless a great deal can be read between the lines, of the *De Excidio Britanniae*, about sixth century Britain in general, and about Maelgwn Gwynedd in particular.

Gildas is addressing himself to a group, probably an élite group, of his contemporaries, and it is clear that Maelgwn is one of these. That is, we can tell from the text that they were both alive together. Gildas, he also tells us, was writing in a time of crisis, so that Maelgwn must have lived through critical times too; but the book makes clear that the attitudes of the two remarkable contemporaries, the king and the historian, could hardly have been more different.

Because he starts with a historical introduction Gildas succeeds in telling us, with some degree of accuracy, how the country came to be in the state it was in the lifetime of Maelgwn. 'Ignorant of the ways of war' it became overrun, when the Romans left, by the Picts and the Scots. The latter probably included the hordes from Ireland which harried North Wales in the century before Maelgwn's time. In this desperate state the High-King who governed the country made a political mistake. He allowed the Saxon tribes to settle, intending to use them as mercenaries. Their rebellion and their overrunning of the country concern other parts of Britain. There is not much evidence that the Saxon advance affected Maelgwn's western kingdom during his lifetime.

One slight exception to this lack of evidence is that it is known that he fought a battle. It was called the battle of Morfa Rhianedd, and it took place on the plain between Deganwy and the Great Orme's Head, partly perhaps the later inundated land which is now Conwy Bay, partly the sandy isthmus on which the town of Llandudno now stands. The battle enters the mythic as well as the historical tale, since it is said that Maelgwn, the victor, left the bodies of his fallen enemies unburied, and it was as a result of this that a disease spread which would prove to be, as we shall see when we move on to the myth, the king's downfall.

It is not certain, of course, that Maelgwn fought the battle of Morfa Rhianedd against the Saxons. Indeed all the evidence is that in his time the centres of Saxon power were some way distant, and it was not until the rise of Mercia, some fifty years later, that Gwynedd came into contact and then conflict with Anglo-Saxon powers. If there were Saxons on Morfa Rhianedd in the first half of the sixth century it is hard to see what they were doing there. Other hints of battles, in local place-names and traditions, probably relate to the period when, in the late ninth century, the kingdom of Mercia was squeezed westwards by the expansion of the rising power of Wessex into the Midlands.

It is quite probable that Maelgwn was fighting his own compatriots. Gildas says of this time (the lull in Saxon advances following the successful resistance led by Ambrosius Aurelianus in the last quarter of the previous century):

External wars may have stopped, but not civil ones . . . Britain has kings, but they are tyrants . . . they wage wars, civil and unjust.

Gildas is generalising here; but since these passages come as an introduction to his specific attack on the kings who were his contemporaries, and since he explicitly says that Maelgwn was the worst of these, we may guess that he had him here in mind; and that the battle of Morfa Rhianedd, therefore, the only battle which the great king is known to have fought, may not have been waged in some noble or patriotic cause. Indeed the closer we come to him the more we begin to wonder how exactly Maelgwn got that aura of greatness.

Let us see, for instance, exactly what Gildas has to say of him.

Gildas deals with five kings of parts of Britain, and he gives them all a hard time. It is part of his purpose, to lament the state of Britain, and no doubt we should take that into account. Nevertheless he clearly feels strongly, and he seems to know a great deal about them. They all seem to have killed their way to their thrones, and in the process undertaken some incestuous and adulterous relations. True to his main theme Gildas blames them for their betrayal of religion. He knocks off four of them with some gusto, but he saves the most heartfelt remonstrances, and the most space, for Maelgwn.

He comes to Maelgwn last, 'last in my list but first in evil', as if he had been saving the best bits for the end. Right from the start he paints a picture of a complex, indeed contradictory person, and we feel the undertow of ambivalence in his tone which convinces us at once that he is addressing himself to a real and in many ways fascinating man.

First he puts into perspective Maelgwn's political position. He addresses him as 'insularis draco', dragon of the island, which is normally taken to mean Anglesey, though it must be said that Gildas certainly does not make this clear. When he refers to 'the island' elsewhere it is always the whole island of Britain, and it may be that he is here implying that Maelgwn's influence is felt throughout the land. Indeed in the same first sentence he accuses his victim of having ousted 'many' of his contemporary kings and taken their lands, implying a position of national high-kingship gained by force of arms. He is, Gildas says, stronger than many both in power and in wickedness. First he generalises about his tendency to 'wallow in his crimes', then sets about specifying exactly what these are. They make pretty shocking reading, and even allowing for the fact that Gildas had a polemical motive for exaggerating, if this was the sort of thing that he is prepared to say went on, then we may wonder what sort of world it was which could permit both ruthless murder and a taste for imported wine to coexist in one man and in this place.

Sticking, he says, 'only to those of your crimes that have been published on the wind far and wide', Maelgwn's first political act was to oust his uncle, the reigning king, in what appears to have been a violent

*The Vardre forms a natural position from which
to defend the river and the coast.*

*The site of the court of Maelgwn Gwynedd overlooks the narrows
at Deganwy with Conwy mountain across the river.*

battle. Having thus seized the throne by force he suffered a brief spell of remorse and became attracted to the life of a monk, to the extent (Maelgwn does nothing by halves) of taking permanent monastic vows. As enthusiastic in devoutness as in vice, he became famous for a time for his sanctity; but his will weakened, and the devil reclaimed him.

His volatile nature, Gildas implies, was his downfall. 'Like a lively foal to whom everything unknown seems attractive,' he whirled from one crime to another. He had already broken his monastic vows by getting married. Not satisfied with that, he became attracted to the wife of another, and that no stranger, but his own nephew. What he wanted he must immediately have, and the fact that two people stood in the way of a fresh marriage (his present wife, and his intended wife's husband) was, to Maelgwn, an inconvenience which had to be removed. He had them both murdered.

Having now killed both his uncle and his nephew, he might well have found himself isolated and vulnerable, but that was not his style. He made a public occasion of his second wedding, and, using the technique of propaganda which, we shall see, was one of the weapons in the armoury of this early military dictator, had it proclaimed that the marriage was legitimate, because the lady was a widow.

Gildas says that he lacked even the excuse of ignorance, since he had a good Christian education. He chooses to be deaf to his conscience, to Biblical commandments, and of course to Gildas.

The question we inevitably ask ourselves is how much we may learn of the real historical king from the accusations in Gildas' clearly polemical, angled diatribe. We may, I think, conclude that at least we know more about Maelgwn than we otherwise would, peering, as in the case of so many other Dark Age figures, into the opaque window of a bit of broken pot. We see, through the medium of Gildas' strong language, a brief glimpse of a soul, a feature quite unknown to archeologists. Since there are some things we can know for certain from Gildas, in a purely factual and non-speculative way, it might be as well to rehearse them.

We know that Gildas regarded him as of special importance. Maelgwn is only one of five kings he deals with, but as N.J. Higham points out, he devotes considerably more space to him than to all the others combined. He tells us at the outset why he does this: he is 'mightier than many . . . in power'. 'The King of all kings had made you higher than almost all the generals of Britain'. Gildas stops short of saying that he is supreme – the words 'than many' and 'almost' are significant. But the clear indication is that he was in a special position of power.

Gildas also makes clear that Maelgwn was well-known. A lot of information about him was already in the public domain. Gildas in fact took the trouble to say that he was broadcasting nothing new. He implies that a lot more personal gossip was in circulation, but agrees to deal only with such crimes as lay in the public sector and had already 'been published on the wind far and wide'. Maelgwn, in fact, made headlines. He was nationally famous.

It also emerges that Maelgwn had an involvement, of a (temporally, at least) benevolent nature, with the emerging religion of Christianity. This is not something that Gildas would have made up, since it did not entirely suit his purpose. We shall see that the tradition also supports this connection.

Interestingly some of the rest of Gildas' specific portrayal of Maelgwn finds a similar echo in later story, though we must not discount the possibility of influence one way or the other, over the centuries during which Gildas' words have been available, and have been copied and reworked. That is, Maelgwn's evident wilfulness and hot-headedness, his dark dealings with members of his family and others, find an echo too in the non-historical tradition. Let us consider for a moment the sources and the nature of this.

'The Story of Taliesin', in which the Maelgwn episode takes place, is first available to us in a mid-16th century manuscript written by Ellis Gruffydd as a *Chronicle of the World*, into which he has inserted various bits of oral tradition and traditional lore. In this case he has anchored a probably very old traditional tale to the sixth century, and hence specifically to Maelgwn. There is no doubt that because of this weakness in our source we lack certainty as to its correct context. We receive the material at one remove, at least, from its probable origin, the perennial oral tradition. It is because of this uncertainty as to its authenticity, in the form in which we have it, that it is sometimes not classed as part of the authentic British material collectively known as The Mabinogion. Lady Charlotte Guest included it, but the later Everyman edition and the Penguin Classics one do not, on the perfectly reasonable ground that it (unlike the rest of that collection) does not occur in either the Red Book of Hergest (a 14th century manuscript now in Jesus College, Oxford), or the White Book of Rhydderch, slightly earlier in the same century, a manuscript which is in the National Library of Wales, which includes almost all the stories now generally known as The Mabinogion.

The American publication of *The Mabinogi*, translated and edited by Patrick K. Ford and published by the University of California Press, however, includes this tale, using Ellis Gruffydd's text, which differs slightly in this version from the one published by Lady Charlotte Guest, suggesting that she was using a different edition of the same source. Between the two we have ample common ground to be sure about what this first non-historical addition to the story of Maelgwn actually says.

King Maelgwn Gwynedd held open court at Christmas in his castle at Deganwy. All the lords of the land had been invited, and Elphin his nephew was among them. The conversation at the court turned to the king's greatness. 'Is there in the whole world a king as great as Maelgwn?' they asked each other, 'or one to whom God has given so many physical and spiritual gifts?' One among these gifts which stood out was the beauty and faithfulness of his wife the queen. They also praised his bards, of whom there were twenty-four present at the court that Christmas.

Elphin however did not conform to this convention of constant praise. Instead, taking the exaggerations literally, he queried their accuracy. Although not worthy to compete with a king, he thought his own wife to be as virtuous, and his own bard to be better.

Maelgwn in effect held these claims to be libellous, and while the testing of the truth of them was in progress, he had Elphin, guilty until proved innocent, thrown into the dungeon. Taliesin enters Maelgwn's world at this point, the poet-prophet who is the centre of the rest of the elaborate tale.

First Taliesin foils an attempt to prove Elphin's wife unfaithful to him. This challenge to his will rekindles Maelgwn's anger, and Elphin is to stay incarcerated until he can make good his second boast, that of the superiority of his bard. Taliesin, foreknowing the sequence of events, makes his way to the court. There, seated inconspicuously and unannounced, he casts a spell over the bards such that they are unable to speak, and instead, in imitation of his actions, stuck out their lips and made on them with their fingers the sound 'Blerwm blerwm'.

This was not the sort of behaviour likely to please a king as wilful and hot-tempered as Maelgwn. At first he assumed they were drunk, and sent a retainer to tell them to remember where they were; when this had no effect he ordered them out of the hall. He also ordered a servant to hit their leader over the head, and this, it seems, had the result of breaking the spell. He spoke.

It was not that they were drunk, he explained, nor was the cause mere foolishness, but a spirit present in the hall had bewitched them. Taliesin is revealed, and brought before the king.

Part of the function of the story is to provide a setting for the verses of Taliesin, which may be at least in part the work of a sixth-century poet of that name. Maelgwn obligingly now provides a cue-line: he asks

St Cybi's church at Holyhead lies within the Roman fort.

The church at Caerhun occupies a corner of the site of the fort of Canovium.

Taliesin what he is and where he comes from.

There follows a long and cryptic poem, the effect of which is that Taliesin claims to be everything and to have been in all places at all times. He is, in other words, the world spirit. Robert Graves makes much of the imagery involved, unravelling the poem in his own fanciful way in a central section of The White Goddess. Maelgwn and his court, however, were simply amazed. He asked Taliesin what he had come for, and was answered again in verse. At length the effect of all this poetry is to create another spell. A great wind rises, a storm so terrible that the king thinks the castle is in danger and hastily has Elphin brought up from the dungeon and presented to Taliesin, who, with another poem, causes his chains to fall off. He then recites a good deal more verse, until, in fact, the story-teller has copied out all the poems attributed to Taliesin which were available to him. There is a horse race, which (with Taliesin's help) Elphin wins; and then more poems. In the last of these Taliesin utters his famous prophecy concerning the destiny of Britain: a serpent would come out of Germany and conquer the land, until the Britons would be prisoners in their own country.

Their lord they shall praise,
Their language they shall keep,
Their land they shall lose –
Except wild Wales.

Lady Charlotte Guest's version, working evidently from a slightly longer text (some of which has been jettisoned, presumably as lacking authenticity, by the American editor), inserts among the poetry a prophecy of Maelgwn's death. Since neither text then goes on to follow this up with the story of Maelgwn's death itself, this is probably inserted from a later, and even less authentic tale.

Although Lady Charlotte Guest does not continue this story in her text, which she tells us she was copying from two separate fragments, she does tell it in full in her notes. Taliesin's curse took the following form. A yellow monster would come from the plain of Rhianedd, to punish the crimes of Maelgwn Gwynedd. Its hair, teeth and eyes were yellow; and this would bring the end of Maelgwn Gwynedd.

The yellow monster she identifies with the yellow plague, of which it was said that whoever came within reach of it would die at once. For this reason (she tells us in her notes) the king retired to the church at Llanrhos hoping for sanctuary there, but in curiosity looked out of the keyhole and saw the monster. The sight of it was enough to kill him. This story she traces back to 'a manuscript by Llywelyn Sion, of

Llangweydd', itself included in 'a manuscript once in the Havod Uchtryd collection'. It must be noted that Lady Charlotte often takes on trust the authenticity of the material which became available to her, and by her own record at least a part of the story of Taliesin was taken from a manuscript which had been in the library of Iolo Morganwg, who has been shown subsequently to have been a great 'improver', or more plainly forger, of Celtic antiquarian material.

The detail about the king dying upon sight of the monster may perhaps come from a mis-translation. Thomas Pennant, in the previous century, had quoted the lines foretelling Maelgwn's death but given the translation as 'Whenever a strange creature arrives on the marsh of Rhianedd, if Maelgwn Gwynedd looks at it, he will die', which has no justification in the text. The disease itself has some corroboration both in the traditional material (this time undoubtedly authentic) and in historical fact. The Welsh Annals, which may quite probably have been written year by year and so, though later copied, date from the actual year they refer to, give for the year 547 the words 'a year of great death in which ended Maelgwn King of Gwynedd. Thus it is said "The long sleep of Maelgwn in the court of Rhos." Then was the yellow plague.' The Triads repeat a reference to 'the yellow plague of Rhos' and its cause and characteristics, but since this collection was compiled (that is, possibly invented) by Iolo Morganwg, it cannot be regarded as supportive evidence.

The plague itself however can be established from other sources. It devastated the sub-Roman world during the mid-sixth century. The plague came from the middle east in the early 540's and had reached the west coast of Britain by the end of that decade. John Davies, in his magisterial *History of Wales*, speculates that the reason it seems to have affected the British but not the English is that the former had links with the Mediterranean, and if this is correct then Maelgwn's death is an ironic consequence of his ability to import eastern Mediterranean wine.

The story of the death of Maelgwn had clearly been current for some time before Lady Charlotte Guest compiled her notes. She wrote in 1848, and in 1829 Thomas Love Peacock had published his *Misfortunes of Elphin*, which launched the whole matter into the realm of an English readership, in which he quotes Taliesin's prophecy and refers to its aftermath, evidently drawing on the same source as Lady Charlotte's notes:

A spectre of the marsh shall rise,
With yellow teeth and hair and eyes,
From whom your king in vain aloof
Shall crouch beneath the sacred roof.
He through the half-closed door shall spy
The Yellow Spectre sweeping by;
To whom the punishment belongs
Of Maelgwn's crimes and Elphin's wrongs.

Though these elements of the later lore surrounding Maelgwn (the prophecy, the yellow monster, the retreat to the church and the spying of the avenging monster through the door) can be traced back thus to some sort of authentic tradition, two favourite and popular stories attached to the name of the historical king have no clear provenance, and so may best be regarded as folk material, perhaps of no very great age.

The tradition that Maelgwn was surrounded by bards and flatterers is traceable, in part, to Gildas, but the fable elaborates on this to state that he held the first eisteddfod. Indeed Bezant Lowe, in *The Heart of Northern Wales* states this as a fact, though as far as provenance is concerned he mentions only 'a poem by Iorwerth Beli' where 'mention is made of a congress of bards and musicians held under the patronage of Maelgwn Gwynedd, on the eminence where Deganwy Castle was built'. The story he then tells may be supposed to come from the same source, though he does not say so.

> On one occasion, Maelgwn, secretly favouring the bards, took care that no boats were available to convey the competitors to the Eisteddfod, which, in this case, was held on Conwy Mountain. They had to swim across the Conwy before the contest, the result being that the musicians' instruments were rendered well-nigh useless, and the poets won all the prizes.

Bezant Lowe does not mention the other fable, but it was so well known in the area that by the 1950's it appeared on a pub sign. Thomas Firbank writes, in the book recording his walking tour of Wales at that time, *A Country of Memorable Honour*:

> The sign showed a crowned king seated on a chair which was befeathered, and about which lapped the waves of the sea.

Briefly, the fable says that Maelgwn held a contest with his rival kings on the sands of Aberdyfi, in which the one who could remain there longest when the tide came in should be the leader. Maelgwn's chair was made of goose-quills and wax, and it floated.

Penmon monastery was originally founded by St Seiriol
during the reign of Maelgwn.

Maelgwn is associated with the religious foundation on Ynys Seiriol,
now known as Puffin Island.

Since he was undoubtedly ruler of North Wales during the mid-6th century, and since our early Christian foundations date to that period, it is reasonable to see Maelgwn as being partly responsible for them. Thus it is said that he endowed the see of Bangor, and gave to St Cybi the site of his monastic church within the enclosure of the Roman fort at Holyhead. Since we may well imagine that a king of North Wales would have control over the defences left by the Romans, it would be likely that the church which lies within the fort of Canovium, on the Conwy river, also lies on a site given by him – or, in this case, his son Rhun, after whom the place is subsequently called, Caer Rhun, Rhun's fort.

Maelgwn is also traditionally associated with the monasteries at Penmon, and on Ynys Seiriol, better known as Puffin Island, where, in some versions of his legend, he is buried. An ancient secular site which is said to have originally been one of his residences is the palace of Llys Euryn, below Bryn Euryn above the Mochdre valley. The present structures at all these places of course belong to later phases of their history.

Maelgwn's legacy to history is mainly that of the founder of a dynasty. From him were descended the two main lines of the House of Gwynedd, that through Rhodri Mawr, from whose line in turn came the great Welsh princes, Owain Gwynedd and the two Llywelyns; and that through Hywel Dda, one of the shoots of which became the House of Tudor. Llywelyn the Great's daughter married into the Mortimer family, the heiress of which later married into the royal English House of York, so that when in due course Henry Tudor confronted Richard III on the battlefield of Bosworth, they were both the remote descendants (as hence is much of the royalty of Europe) of this towering Dark Age king.

He casts a long shadow. Yet though we thus know something of what, by his power and strength of personality, he achieved in affecting the course of British history, we also know a bit about what he might have done, given those attributes, but failed to. He did not use his considerable power to unite the British kingdoms in the period of post-Roman decline. Indeed we find his son Rhun becoming famous for fighting his own people, first being invaded by, then marching against in retribution, a consortium of northern princes. Maelgwn did not exert his political influence and personal astuteness to anticipate, and pre-empt, the westward spread of the Angles and the northern spread of the Saxons. During his lifetime the latter were expanding their kingdom dramatically from their base in the Isle of Wight, the former spreading from their east-coast kingdoms of Deira and Bernicia up the river Trent, from which they would in due course meet the Severn. Maelgwn did not enable the rise of a strong independent Britain.

It is a long-standing thesis of mine that the Anglo-Saxon invaders were facilitated in consolidating their hold on central Britain because Maelgwn Gwynedd was facing the wrong way. The history of his ancestors' struggle with invaders from across the Irish Sea, in the aftermath of which he grew up, together with the placing of his main fortress on this seaward-looking bluff above Deganwy made him look to the west for enemies, when they were there in the east behind him all the time. Thinking himself secure, he indulged his extravagant tastes and vices. Maelgwn had the power and the political cohesion to repulse or at least contain the new invaders; he was simply not aware of the threat they represented.

Llywelyn the Great

North Wales has never been a clearly-defined political unit. It consisted in the Middle Ages of two kingdoms, Gwynedd and Powys, each subdivided again into 'cantrefi', a unit of, theoretically, a hundred towns, equivalent to the English hundred which once formed the division of a county. By Llywelyn's time the basic unit of administration was a yet-smaller subdivision, the 'cwmwd' or commote, of which there were two or three to each cantref. This gave considerable flexibility to the governing of North Wales, and it must be said that there were few occasions in its history when the whole area was under the control of one man.

One such, however, was the reign of Rhodri Mawr. The royal line founded by Maelgwn Gwynedd, the hero of the last chapter, had survived, by the 9th century, in the person of Merfyn Frych, 'the freckled', who married the heiress of the royal house of Powys. Their son Rhodri was thus in due course to inherit the thrones of the two kingdoms.

It was unusual, in history, for Gwynedd and Powys to be united. Normally they were embroiled in rivalry, if not in war. Their combination brought into being a political force which had to be taken seriously.

Rhodri did not stop there. By judicious marriage he gained control too of a large part of South Wales. He was a forceful leader and staunch defender of his almost unwieldy territories. He won several notable battles, and in the end he died fighting.

Rhodri had trouble on all sides, from the start, and a less determined man would have let Wales disintegrate. Instead he held it together and, most significantly for our present purpose, handed on to his successors a country with a clearer identity than it had ever had.

To a large extent Rhodri lived in a time of change, when old conventions and concepts were being overturned by new ones. For some two hundred years, by 844 when he became king of Gwynedd, both

Cymryd Point, on the river Conwy, is said by early sources to be the site of the battle of 'Dial Rhodri', 'Rhodri's Revenge.

Tomen-y-Rhodwydd ring fort near Llanarmon was built by Owain Gwynedd in the 12th century.

Gwynedd and Powys had had to reckon with their powerful neighbour the Anglian kingdom of Mercia. Now both they and the Mercians had to contend with new enemies. In the south the West Saxons formed a major threat to them all; and in the west and north both Welsh and Anglo-Saxon kingdoms started to be seriously plagued by Vikings.

Rhodri established himself at once by scoring a major victory over the Vikings in Anglesey, in 856. He went on to try to combat his second enemy, since Wessex had overrun Powys in 828. The kingdom still retained its identity, since Rhodri had become king of it in 855, and evidently its people had not given up hope of regaining their independence. But with both Mercia and Wessex claiming Powys, and the former pressed westwards by the latter, it became more of a struggle. Rhodri went to war against the Mercians in 878, and was defeated. Thus he died fighting.

He died fighting for his lost inheritance of a largely unified Wales. In doing so he bequeathed to his heirs that ideal, and this inspired his son Anarawd, who successfully rebuffed an incursion of the Mercians into North Wales, at a battle on the Conwy river in 880. So conscious were they of the significance of this reversal of his defeat, two years after his death, that the Welsh named the victory *Dial Rhodri*, Rhodri's Revenge, his ideals and his achievements evidently still forming a motivating force.

He bequeathed to the future, in fact, much more than this, by ensuring that from him a much longer progression of the idea of Wales would continue. During his time the roots of Welsh literature, and hence of an identifiable Welsh culture took shape. The poetic cycles started to be written down, preserving the old heroic traditions and values which were already a part of the nation's identity to form the spine of the traditional culture, and equally significantly the Welsh Annals, on which we still rely for many of our facts, were compiled, indicating that a country with a sense of its own history had come into being.

Rhodri, himself descended from two royal lines, and married into another, was in a position to give validity to the succession of rulers of Wales. From him descended two important lines of princes. From his son Cadell came that of the rulers of South Wales, the law-maker Hywel Dda, and later The Lord Rhys, whose daughter Gwenllian married Llywelyn the Great's lieutenant, Ednyfed Fychan, their descendants adopting the name Tewdor, which eventually, as Tudor, became their family name. Thus it was that Henry Tudor, great-grandson of an Anglesey squire, could legitimately claim descent from the royal line of Wales, with Rhodri forming its nexus.

Basingwerk, now the ruins of an abbey, was the site of a major battle in the 12th century.

Rhuddlan was originally a castle of the Norman marcher lords, extended in the 13th century by Edward I.

It is with the other line of descent from that focal point that we are mainly concerned here. From Rhodri's elder son, Anarawd, stem the later rulers of Gwynedd, at first unremarkable, but culminating in the 12th century with two notably effective kings of Gwynedd, Cynan and his son Gruffudd.

Wales had become disunited again, but through them a measure of unity was restored. Gruffudd ap Cynan's son, as we shall see, Owain Gwynedd, was a major figure of Welsh history. Llywelyn the Great was his grandson.

To understand the situation into which Wales had in the meantime fallen we have to understand the Welsh tradition of inheritance. When Rhodri died in 878 it would not have been viewed as correct, and so would not have gained general acquiescence, if the whole of the kingdom he had built up had been inherited by one man. The Welsh custom was to divide the deceased's property between his sons. Primogeniture was not a concept they had acquired. This, though thoroughly in keeping with Celtic notions of fairness and equality, has given rise to considerable problems over the centuries, such as the breaking up of farms until our countryside is seamed with boundary walls and dotted with small-holdings. In the Middle Ages it meant that if a ruler were to become powerful he had to do so by the forceful eviction of his relatives, and this in turn left in the background the resentment of the dispossessed, at any time likely to break out into a dangerous family feud.

A partial solution to this problem was judicious marriage. It was through intermarriage between houses that Rhodri had built up his large kingdom, first through his parents' and then through his own. If he had had a daughter he might even have increased it. But he had two sons.

It is thus that on the death of Rhodri in 878 two separate lines of rule descended, one in North Wales and one in the south. His son Anarawd, as we have seen, became king of Gwynedd and Powys, while Cadell, his other son, inherited the southern kingdoms. His son in turn, Hywel Dda, extended these southern territories by marrying into the royal house of Dyfed.

This is significant, from our point of view, because of the great power which it gave to the kings of southern Wales, the descendants of Hywel Dda, which enabled them to interfere with the rights of their cousins in the north. In fact for a time Wales was effectively ruled as a whole by the kings of the south. Notable among these was Gruffudd ap Llywelyn, who not only unified Wales for the first and only time but expanded its borders into Cheshire and Shropshire.

*Dolwyddelan is a castle of the independent Welsh princes,
probably built by Llywelyn the Great.*

Gruffudd achieved his unique position by ruthless determination. In the process of seizing Gwynedd he killed its king, Iago, the great-great-grandson of Anarawd. Iago's son, the rightful heir of Gwynedd, Cynan, fled to Ireland.

Dublin was then, of course, a Viking city. Cynan's choice of refuge indicates that relations between North Wales and the Norsemen must have been improving. His stay there brought the two nations firmly into alliance, a historical chance which thereafter had a radical effect on the future of Gwynedd.

Cynan in fact married the daughter of the Viking king of Dublin. It was thus that his son Gruffudd was both heir to the kingdom of Gwynedd and half-Norse. The process by which he re-established his hold on Gwynedd is confused, but it is generally agreed to have been with Viking help. What definitely resulted was that then North Wales, free for the first time for three hundred years from the ravages of the Norsemen, became the stable, cultured, prosperous place for which it had always had the potential. Gruffudd lived to be 82, and when he died in 1137 he left to his son, Owain Gwynedd, an extended secure kingdom.

Churches were built of stone then, replacing the wooden structures set up by the dark age saints. Monasteries were founded on a coastline at last free from raids. Owain built castles along his borders, confronting, in their own terms, the Marcher lords. Tomen y Rhodwydd is a good example of Owain's work, standing as it does near Llanarmon in a territory often, in history, in the hands of the Earl of Chester.

Owain was a king who had to be taken seriously by the English monarchy. Henry II fought a pitched battle against him at Basingwerk, in which both sides came off badly, and the two kings, having tested each other's strength, decided to negotiate a peace. It was the first of many such treaties, and it marks the start of a new age of politics and diplomacy.

That treaty also defined the status of Gwynedd, in that Owain was allowed to rule over it as an independent realm, provided that he did not encroach into the territory of the Earl of Chester, that stretch of what is, and was, traditionally thought of as Wales, which lies between Chester and the Norman castle town of Rhuddlan. This, precisely, is the immediate background against which we have to see the momentous events of the reign of his grandson, Llywelyn the Great.

Owain was not a man to be content with his barren mountain kingdom. He wanted the rich plains too. During the 1160's Henry was in trouble in London, having jeopardised his throne by his quarrel with the church, in the person of the Archbishop of Canterbury, Thomas à

Only fragments now remain of the castle at Deganwy demolished and rebuilt more than once in the struggle between the Welsh princes and Plantagenet kings.

Trefriw village hall is traditionally said to stand on the site of Llywelyn's court.

Becket. Owain, evidently politically opportunist, took Rhuddlan castle and from it controlled the land as far as the river Dee. Henry could not, for all his problems, risk the fall of Chester, and he came to Wales with a massive force. After some skirmishes, which left the matter undecided, the Welsh weather (not for the first or last time) entered the war on the side of the natives, and Henry's army got so battered by rain on the Berwyns that he moved them back into England. After that he tried diplomacy rather than war, a course facilitated by the confusion which followed the death of Owain Gwynedd.

Owain does not seem to have designated a successor, possibly because it seemed clear to him that his kingdom would be inherited by his eldest son, Iorwerth. When Owain died, in November 1170, his kingdom appears to have been divided among his sons. Owain had married twice, the second time to his cousin. We find the forceful son of that marriage emerging early as the main contester for the throne of Gwynedd. In the year following his father's death the Chronicles tell us that he slew his elder brother. That, we may feel, was a good start. In 1173 he ousted his brother Maelgwn from Anglesey, driving him into exile in Ireland. By 1174 he had 'gained possession of all Gwynedd, after expelling all his brothers and uncles'. He also imprisoned the unfortunate Maelgwn, at which point it seems another brother, Cynan, also died, leaving Dafydd in complete control.

Where, in the meantime, was Iorwerth, the natural heir? It seems that he had (perhaps wisely) moved to south Wales, since we find him in 1172 having problems with the king of England in the Cardiff area, in 1173 besieging the city and then the castle of Caerleon, and in 1175 being given those possessions in a peace settlement made by King Henry.

Dafydd was at the same time consolidating his position. Having dealt with the main branch of his family, the sons of Owain's first wife, he now turned, tidying up the situation, on his brother by the same mother, whom he had apparently so far spared. He accused him of treachery 'for seeking a portion of his patrimony from him' and threw him into prison in shackles. This backfired somewhat, as Rhodri escaped, perhaps offering a warning that it is better to kill them outright. That same year Dafydd launched into wider diplomacy, marrying the half-sister of the king of England, Emma, the illegitimate daughter of Geoffrey of Anjou, 'believing that because of that he would be allowed to maintain his territory in peace'.

He had not, however, exactly set up the ideal conditions for a peaceful reign.

In 1194 the contemporary members of the dispossessed families got together and moved against Dafydd. A battle took place near Aberconwy, at the mouth of the Conwy river. It seems more than likely that Iorwerth had possessions in the Conwy valley, a curious oversight on the part of the ruthless Dafydd. Llywelyn ap Iorwerth, then aged twenty-two, was the leader of the coup, but he did not behave at all in the manner of his uncle. He allowed Dafydd to retire to his lands near Ellesmere (given him as a wedding gift by the king of England), and for a time he shared the ruling of Gwynedd with those others who had joined him in gaining it, his cousins the sons of Cynan and Rhodri.

We have one tantalising insight into the formative years of this figure who was to become one of the most powerful of the historical personages of Wales. 'Giraldus Cambrensis', Gerald the Welshman, made a progress through Wales in 1188, in the retinue of Archbishop Baldwin, the purpose of which was to raise recruits for the Third Crusade. He kept a detailed diary of his journey. From Bangor travelling northwards 'We continued our journey on the sea coast, confined on one side by steep rocks, and by the sea on the other, towards the river Conwy . . . ' Ruminating on the tomb of Owain which he had been shown in Bangor, he adds an aside which it will be worth quoting in full:

I shall pass over in silence what was done by the sons of Owain in our days, after his death, or while he was dying, who, from the wicked desire of reigning, totally disregarded the ties of fraternity; but I shall not omit mentioning another event which occurred likewise in our days. Owain, son of Gruffudd, prince of North Wales, had many sons, but only one legitimate, namely, Iorwerth Drwyndwn, which in Welsh means flat-nosed, who had a son named Llywelyn. This young man, being only twelve years of age, began, during the period of our journey, to molest his uncles Dafydd and Rhodri, the sons of Owain by Christiana, his cousin-german; and although they had divided amongst themselves all North Wales, except the land of Cynan, and although Dafydd, having married the sister of King Henry II, by whom he had one son, was powerfully supported by the English, yet within a few years the legitimate son, destitute of lands or money (by the aid of divide vengeance), bravely expelled from North Wales those who were born in public incest, though supported by their own wealth and by that of others, leaving them nothing but what the liberality of his own mind and the counsel of good men from pity suggested: a proof that adulterous and incestuous persons are displeasing to God.

A number of points may be made about this interesting passage. Firstly the account of Llywelyn's eventual success was clearly added with hindsight. We know that Gerald, disappointed in his ecclesiastical career, had retired in the late 1210's till his death in 1223 to add to and rework his earlier writings. It is possible, indeed likely, therefore, that this evident insert was added at a time when Llywelyn ap Iorwerth was at the height of his powers. It is possible further that it was actually written to please the powerful ruler of much of Wales, which it evidently succeeded in doing, if Llywelyn's own prophecy concerning Gerald is authentic:

> So long as Wales shall stand by the writings of the chroniclers and by the songs of the bards shall his noble deed be praised throughout all time.

This would explain the emphasis on legitimacy, and the incestuous (and therefore invalid) nature of Owain's second marriage. Gerald had just recorded an event at Bangor which he no doubt witnessed. Owain's tomb was in a vault in front of the high altar in spite of the fact that 'on account of his public incest with his cousin-german, (he) had died excommunicated by the blessed martyr St Thomas'. Baldwin, according to another manuscript, found the entombment within the cathedral of an excommunicant incorrect, and, Gerald continues, the Bishop of Bangor was 'enjoined to seize a proper opportunity of removing his body from the church'.

Another point of interest is that Cynan was apparently, alone among Dafydd's brothers, allowed to reign over part of Gwynedd, a reason perhaps for Llywelyn's tolerance of the rule of his sons over parts of it even after his seizure of power.

Thirdly we may note that at the time of the journey Llywelyn himself, if our other information is correct, was fourteen rather than the highly-precocious twelve which Gerald designates him. Fourteen was an age by which young nobles might well be expected to take part in active service and political life.

Richard II, for instance, was fourteen (a little less than two hundred years later) when he successfully led his troops against the rebellious peasants during their famed Revolt. Richard's father, the Black Prince, had won the crucial victory at Crecy at the age of sixteen. Since Llywelyn's father Iorwerth had, it seems, died at about the time of his birth, he must have been used, from early childhood, to an acceptance of his role in an adult world.

Yet another point of interest is Gerald's mention of Iorwerth's nick-name, Flat-Nose. It seems that he had at some time suffered a broken nose, 'for which defect,' opines W. Llewelyn Williams, in his 1908 edition of Gerald's 'Itinerary', 'he was deemed unfit to preside over the

Only a bank in a field indicates the site of Llywelyn's great court at Aberffraw.

Ewloe was one of the castles built by Llywelyn to protect the approaches to his principality.

principality of North Wales and was deprived of his rightful inheritance, which was seized by his brother David . . . ' John Davies, in *A History of Wales*, supports this speculation – 'kings had to be without blemish' – in the current literature. It does not seem likely, given Dafydd's behaviour, that he would have needed such an excuse. If tradition rather than ruthless force had been his political style, his own illegitimacy would have been as powerful an argument against him.

It is not certain to us, now, of course, to whom the mores of the Middle Ages are inevitably a strange land, to what extent a broken nose would weigh against a cousin-marriage, at that time regarded (as we have evidence) as incest. We can only judge the motivations of those concerned by their behaviour.

Gerald refers to 'the land of Cynan' and, in his next chapter, 'the land of the sons of Cynan', those, that is, who had assisted Llywelyn in his overthrow of their uncle Dafydd. These were Gruffudd and Maredudd. The latter was evidently ruler of Llŷn, since Llywelyn drove him from there in 1201, 'because' (say the chronicles) 'of his treachery'. But he could not do that, evidently, until the former had died. He appears to have ruled another part of Gwynedd, possibly the Conwy area, since we find him, near his death, taking the habit of the Cistercian order there. According to one of the chronicles he was an exceptionally popular man 'because of the abundance of his gifts and his gentleness and his goodness', which perhaps explains why Llywelyn did not simply find him guilty of treachery and expel him.

He died at Aberconwy in the year 1200. It was not until then that Llywelyn's supremacy began. He was then aged twenty-eight.

Besides the reference by Gerald to his precocious start we know little of Llywelyn's life before his appearance on the world stage. It is widely assumed that after his father's death he was brought up among his mother's kin in northern Powys. The legend that he was born in Dolwyddelan castle is probably not true. Even if the castle referred to is the older one of which there are signs near to the present keep, there is no evidence that it was built by, or the possession of, his father Iorwerth. In the 1170's, the time of Llywelyn's birth, we hear of Iorwerth seldom but always in connection with south Wales.

As far as I am able to determine it was Sir John Wynne, in his *History of the Gwydir Family* who is to blame for the Dolwyddelan legend, and also for the notion that it was Iorwerth's broken nose which debarred him from monarchy. Sir John is not always right, though often this was not his fault. He worked carefully from a wide collection of authentic documents, but had no means of checking the accuracy of their information.

After the death of Owain, Iorwerth or Edward, his son, being thought unfit to govern by reason of the deformity of his face, Dafydd, his brother, became prince in his father's room.

I find that Iorwerth Drwyndwn or Edward with the broken nose, being put from the government of the Principality, had assigned him for his part of his father's inheritance the hundreds of Nanconwy and Ardudwy. He dwelt at the castle of Dolwyddelan where it is thought credibly his son, Llywelyn the Great or Prince Llywelyn, was born . . .

Although it is likely that Iorwerth had such a territory by right, it seems unlikely that he occupied it, and there is no certain evidence of a castle of his time. Sir John then correctly points out that at least at the time of Gerald's journey Dafydd was not in complete control in North Wales, since the Archbishop's party was greeted in Anglesey by Rhodri, who had not only escaped from his brother's prison but repossessed some of his patrimony. He then says that Rhodri 'had in his court Llywelyn, the son of Iorwerth or Edward, his nephew', though the standard text of Gerald's Itinerary makes no mention of this.

It is not in fact entirely clear which side Rhodri was on, in Llywelyn's coup against Dafydd. In any case he died in 1195, leaving further room for the expansion of Llywelyn's power. This he wisely shared with those who had helped him obtain it. Gruffydd, the elder of the two sons of Cynan, ruled Anglesey, Arfon, Arllechwedd and Llŷn. Maredudd, the younger brother, probably governed Meirionnydd and Eifionydd. Llywelyn himself ruled east of the Conwy. It is interesting to see how gradual was the process by which he came to be undisputed ruler of almost all of Wales.

In Dafydd's former kingdom on the English side of the Conwy river he had his mother's kinsmen, the princes of northern Powys, as neighbours, and this must have been to his advantage in that place of troubled borders. Amazingly the humbled Dafydd was allowed to retain three castles, according to the Chronicles, though they do not say which these were. Perhaps they were minor wooden structures. This leniency, however, threatened Llywelyn's security, and in 1197 he finally exiled his uncle to his Ellesmere lands, together with his wife Emma (of the English royal house) and their son Owain.

The year 1199 is a crucial one in the development of the story of Llywelyn. In January he took the bold step of attacking and occupying the castle at Mold – bold, because this was very much a buffer between the lands of the Welsh and the important Marcher castles of Chester and Hawarden, its loss thus a threat to them. At the time, in January, it may have seemed that the king of England was unlikely to respond with invasion to the loss of one small castle. Richard I was in Britain at the time, but this was rare, since he spent much of his reign far-distant on crusade. When at home he had, as a result, much work to do controlling over-powerful forces in his realm. It was doing so that he died, besieging a hostile baron, shot by a bolt from the castle. That was in April.

What happened then was crucial to Llywelyn, since King John was a king of a very different kind. He himself was a Marcher lord, and he knew both how the Welsh temperament worked and how important it was to take account of it. Although his reign was to be plagued with trouble, due largely to his own ruthless and autocratic character, he spent a large part of it dealing, in one way or another, with Wales.

Although with the death of Gruffydd ap Cynan his power had expanded considerably, since he now ruled Arfon, Anglesey and Arllechwedd, and because of his kinship ties remained on good terms with the men of northern Powys, there was, in the early years of the 13th century, a growing problem further south, in the person of Gwen-wynwyn, prince of southern Powys. These two great leaders were in fact destined to spend much of their lives forming a limiting factor to each other's power. It was a situation which could not be lost on the astute King John.

In 1202 Llywelyn attempted a decisive move. He mustered a considerable army and moved into southern Powys. This turned out, however, not to be the solution he intended. He could not conclude the matter without the full consent of his kinsmen and supporters, and one, his uncle from his family in Powys, would not go with him. The latter suffered the confiscation of almost all his lands as a result, allowing Llywelyn to spread his rule as far south as Bala, but Gwenwynwyn survived. Peace was arranged by the clergy, and Llywelyn went home.

To begin with King John supported Llywelyn against his rival. Evidently Powys was felt, on first appraisal, to be more of a threat to the English border than Gwynedd. There is no doubt that Gwenwynwyn was an ambitious man. It was his misfortune that he was perhaps not quite as ambitious as Llywelyn.

For a time a delicate balancing act went on, the king favouring the one rival until his power became excessive, then switching his implied allegiance to the other. Sir John Lloyd, in his definitive *History of Wales*, sums up the classic situation: 'His aim was to divide and to disintegrate, to checkmate the designs of the more formidable chiefs by favouring their rivals . . . ' Llywelyn too, every bit a match for anyone in diplomatic acumen, played this high-risk game.

Cricieth castle, with its 'D'-shaped towers, shows a transition in form of castle-building from square towers to round.

*Dolbadarn castle, in the area of Llanberis,
is Llywelyn's first round-towered castle.*

For a time he was quite clearly winning. The first decade of the 13th century saw him basking in the sunlight of the English king's approval. He took an oath of loyalty to King John in 1201. In 1204 he went to do him homage. So effective were these marks of friendship that that same year the king offered the prince the hand of his daughter. The auspicious marriage of Llywelyn and Princess Joan took place in the spring of 1205. It is a delicate point of irony that John then gave them as a dowery those same Ellesmere lands which Henry II had given as a dowery to his uncle Dafydd. The latter had died in 1203, and the estates reverted to the Crown.

All this paid off handsomely for Llywelyn. In 1207 Gwenwynwyn was arrested by the king at Shrewsbury, and Llywelyn, taking his cue, annexed his territory. This sent shivers of fear throughout Wales, and castles were burnt rather than risk his possessing them. Nevertheless Llywelyn was now unstoppable. It is probably about that point that King John realised his mistake.

He had in fact by then made several. It was a mistake to dispossess William de Breos, head of a powerful Marcher family ruling Brecon, Radnor, Builth and Abergavenny. He and his wife and son took refuge in Ireland. When the king came in 1210 on an Irish campaign he took the opportunity to return to Wales. It was probably that move which set in motion the chain of events which was to lead Llywelyn into war.

Something, at any rate, set off, that year, hostilities between Llywelyn and the Earl of Chester. Whatever the underlying cause, the immediate excuse was the question of Deganwy castle. This, occupying the same hill as the seat of Maelgwn Gwynedd, dark age ancestor of Wales' princes, had originally been built (in its medieval form) by Robert of Rhuddlan, a Norman Marcher lord, in the 1070's. This, though no trace of it survives, was substantial enough to be remarked on by Giraldus, when he crossed the Conwy with Archbishop Baldwin in 1188. Sometime before 1210, the year with which we are concerned, Llywelyn himself had built a castle there. That, however, he had by then destroyed, 'for fear', the Chronicle says, 'of the king'. In 1210 the Earl of Chester rebuilt it.

Diplomat though he was, Llywelyn was by no means the sort of man to take such an act of provocation lightly. He at once 'ravaged' the earl's land. A number of curious points arise, however, at this point, which we must consider.

Why, before 1210, was Llywelyn so distrustful of his father-in-law that he pulled down one of his own castles, well within his controlled territory, for fear that the king might use it against him? There is no doubt that John had started to behave strangely. His unpredictable outbursts of violence are well illustrated by the de Breos case. The Chronicles give no motive other than jealousy and hatred; perhaps they had simply grown too powerful. Dispossession and exile are bad enough, but the king then proceeded to make matters infinitely worse. When William escaped to Wales he captured his wife and son in Ireland, brought them back to Windsor, where he put them to a 'horrible' or 'unmerciful' death.

If Llywelyn was so nervous of the king before that he thought it prudent to destroy Deganwy castle, how much more must he have feared invasion when Deganwy castle was rebuilt, well within the territory he then controlled, in front of his eyes, by Norman hands.

One of King John's responses was to restore Gwenwynwyn. Such sudden reversals of favour are not unusual in history, particularly at this time of the Middle Ages, and though we may be surprised at the ease with which a leader may be thrown into prison and then suddenly become an ally in war, or vice versa, we should perhaps reflect that in our own times too it has occasionally been a short step from being imprisoned as a terrorist or traitor to being guest of honour at a state banquet at Buckingham Palace. Though it is difficult for us to understand such reconciliations, how Gwenwynwyn could swallow his resentment, we have to accept that politics works thus. The trick is to survive.

Llywelyn's attacks on Norman border lands caused the mustering of a royal army. Gwenwynwyn was not the only disaffected Welsh leader to join it. Many were ready, at that time, to turn against Llywelyn. He for his part saw this coming, and reacted with discretion. It has been remarked many times that one of the great strengths of the people of North Wales in times of war was their ability to disappear. The Romans marched in ordered ranks against them, and found to their irritation that they weren't there. Similarly the several great armies mustered at Chester were puzzled to find that they could march into Wales unopposed. No army manned the border to repel them. No one was there at all.

This technique was due to several factors, and had several results. The Welsh knew quite well that they would be no match for a trained militia in a pitched battle. On the few occasions they had tried it (as when Llywelyn's grandfather Owain Gwynedd took on the forces of Henry II at Basingwerk) it had not been entirely successful. What the Welsh had, which their neighbours lacked, was complete mobility, in the sense that all their valuables could be rounded up and herded out of reach. They were not an agrarian economy. As a pastoral people they had no problem about moving.

What this meant as far as the invader was concerned was not just that there was no-one to fight, there was nothing to eat either. It was assumed, rashly, that the vast army now moving into North Wales could be supplied by plunder of the lands they went through. But instead they came all the way to Deganwy without resistance, but without provisions either.

Llywelyn had been right in his perception of the immediate danger to him of the rebuilding of Deganwy castle. King John and his army with their Welsh supporters went straight to it. This would have made some sense if he had arranged to be supplied by sea, but it seems the expedition was badly-planned and ill-conceived.

> And the king came, according to his plan, to the castle of Deganwy. And there the host suffered lack of food to such an extent that an egg was sold for a penny-halfpenny; and they found the flesh of their horses as good as the best dishes. And because of that the king, having lost many of his men, about Whit Sunday returned in shame to England without having fulfilled aught of his mission.

So the Welsh Chronicle reports. The English equivalent (the 'Barnwell annalist') is equally explicit:

> The king of England led an army into Wales against Llywelyn, but returned very quickly because the Welsh, fearing his advance, withdrew with their property into the mountains, so that the English army was beset with hunger.

That was at the end of May. By August he was back again, this time with an even larger force, and, the English chronicle specifies, 'with plenty of supplies'.

This time too he came a different way. In July he was at Oswestry, and it was probably there that he gathered his host. This meant that instead of confronting the tidal Conwy at Deganwy he could cross the barrier of that river higher up, and so make the breakthrough of entering the heartland of Gwynedd. Most probably he crossed the hills by the line of the old Roman road, and so came down to Aber, which he made his base. He had a quarrel to settle with the bishop of Bangor at the time, and sent a party of men to burn the city and capture the bishop, who saved himself with a ransom of two hundred falcons.

With the king now deep inside his territory Llywelyn was prompted to urgent action. Evidently his guerrilla troops and tactics were no match for

Castell-y-Bere, in the Dysynni valley, is perhaps Llywelyn's grandest and most impressive castle.

The magnificent stone base of Princess Joan's coffin is still to be seen in the church porch at Beaumaris.

this considerable army; he had seen Bangor burnt. The Conwy river had not, as before, protected him from invasion. He decided to use his secret weapon.

Then Joan, Llywelyn's wife, went to treat with her father, the king of England.

In the words of one chronicle, and another puts it more fully:

And then Llywelyn, being unable to suffer the king's rage, sent his wife, the king's daughter, . . . to make peace with the king on whatever terms he could.

The terms were not good for the Welsh side, in spite of the influence of their intermediary. Llywelyn lost the right to his dominions east of the Conwy, and suffered a fine of twenty thousand cattle and forty horses. No wonder that 'the king returned victorious with great joy to England'.

In the process almost all the Welsh princes had made peace with the king, and with their help he seized the territory of those who did not. His lieutenants started building him a strong castle at Aberystwyth. This, however, as far as the Welsh leaders were concerned, was a step too far. Evidently they had assumed that once having made peace they would be allowed to carry on much as before. The sight of the castle going up impressed on them that John was not a distant benevolent ruler. Some of them changed their minds and pulled it down.

Evidently there were other castles being built, and John's presence exerted from them. It was the behaviour of 'the king's men who had been left in the new castles' which caused Llywelyn, and his fellow princes, to resist. Now united, they took by storm all the king's castles in Gwynedd (presumably the recently erected invasion forts, probably made of wood), except those two venerable stone-built structures, Rhuddlan and Deganwy. King John still held these, and with them something of a grip on Wales.

Oddly enough Llywelyn (and presumably his wife) spent the Easter of 1212 with his father-in-law at Cambridge. This was during the peace and immediately before the insurrection, and Sir John Lloyd suggests that it might have been a causal factor. Having seen the state of affairs at the English court 'Llywelyn thus learnt that he had no reason to fear a second invasion . . . ' King John was, to put it mildly, in a weak position. He was barely clinging to his throne, largely in the power of hostile and determined barons. That would have been evident at Easter. It was the end of June when the Welsh leaders revolted.

John was in the north. On 28th June he was at Durham. Llywelyn had recovered the borderland by the time he came to Chester. It looked for a time as if Llywelyn had miscalculated, and an invasion was imminent. But the king had to keep an eye over his shoulder. Letters had been sent to him revealing a plot by the barons to betray him during the Welsh campaign. Whether this was itself a plot in Llywelyn's favour, or whether the Welsh rising was a part of that conspiracy, were both possibilities which must have occurred to him. At any rate on 16th August he called the campaign off.

Llywelyn was now in secure control. Early in 1213 Deganwy and Rhuddlan were taken. By 1214 King John, threatened with civil war, was turning to the Welsh princes for their support. He did not get it. Instead Llywelyn and Gwenwynwyn allied themselves with the northern rebels. Llywelyn took Shrewsbury, and the next year pressed on into South Wales. By December 1215 he had taken all the royal centres there. It was a mild winter, so he was able to campaign right through it. On 26th December he pressed on into mid Wales, taking Cardigan and Cilgerran. Once again the security of a political situation was reinforced by marriage. Reginald de Breos, recently inheriting his family's territory around Hereford from his brother, married Llywelyn's daughter, ensuring peace along the mid-Wales border.

Llywelyn, then aged 43, was the undisputed ruler of a nation. In 1216 he called a Parliament at Aberdovey, at which, with remarkable sagacity, he shared out the districts of Wales among his fellow-princes, keeping nothing for himself. His position was that of overlord of them all. Under the protection of his personal power life in North Wales was allowed a brief period of blossom.

What, we may wonder, was it actually like, to live in North Wales in the time of Llywelyn, the end of the 12th and start of the 13th century? Often such questions are merely rhetorical; but this time, as it happens, we know quite a lot about it. We know this largely thanks to Giraldus, who wrote a 'Description' of Wales as well as his remarkable 'Itinerary', and also thanks to detailed and scholarly work, making use of charters, letters and court rolls, and also of the chronicles to which, in this chapter, I often refer, published in such books as David Stephenson's 'The Governance of Gwynedd', University of Wales Press 1984, and Sir John Lloyd's 'A History of Wales' published in 1912.

This was a land in which there was almost no concept of a town. The nearest that North Wales had seen to urbanisation was the Roman camps. Their surrounding shanty towns gave them, when they were in use, an urban nature, and such might have been seen once at Caernarfon. Whereas at Chester the Roman fort had developed into a city, and elsewhere along the border, at Shrewsbury, for instance, and Hereford, Norman lordships bringing with them the hierarchy of knights and retainers had developed administrative centres, Llywelyn's courts and castles were based more on the model of a Roman villa, homesteads in a rural land.

North Wales' essential ruralness at this time was based on its agricultural system. There was very little cultivated land. The ordinary person in Llywelyn's kingdom was a shepherd or herdsman. He tended his flocks on the upper slopes of the valleys, looking down on a sea of oak and birch. He is a light and agile man, probably bare-foot, dressed in a cloth resembling canvas, not (the chronicler Walter Map observes) in wool or fur. His beard is shaved, but he wears a fine moustache. A meat-eater by habit, he takes great care of his teeth, which he polishes with green hazel. His hair is cut short, as indeed is that of his wife, hers however being covered with a veil. He is, we are told, exceptionally quick-minded, both cunning and witty, fond of jokes, and, however humble, eloquent and forthright in any company. He has a compulsive love of music and readily takes part in choral singing. At home he eats frugally, but puts a high value on hospitality, and his home is open to any traveller. His home contains little furniture, and no ornament. Simple and limited dishes are served on grass and rushes, and rushes form the beds too, with a coarse cloth blanket, where the household all sleep together. That is, when the harp-playing and tale-telling has ended. The fire burns all night.

There is a little arable land, for instance on Anglesey, which has already earned the nickname 'Môn Mam Cymru', mother of Wales because it is said that it can provide enough corn for all the country's inhabitants; and in the catchment area of Chester, the cleared and cultivated land which once formed the Roman 'prata', supplying the large number of men and horses garrisoned in the legionary headquarters. The former area was always vulnerable to attack and important to defend. The latter for much of this time under the control of the Normans. From a military and political point of view the significance of the largely pastoral economy was that the resulting mobility gave the Welsh an advantage in invasion. They did not even have houses to burn down, but simple and serviceable huts made out of branches. They planted neither orchards nor gardens. Their wealth lay in stock, so it was mobile. Thus when invaders came they found not only nothing to destroy, but nothing to commandeer either.

Not surprisingly, given this social economy, Wales was not at that time a trading nation. Some timber, we know, was exported to the rising

Along with Aberconwy, Cymer Abbey on the Mawddach was one of the two great monasteries patronised by Llywelyn.

border towns and beyond; some grain and cloth imported. But on the whole there was no manufacture and hardly any commerce. It is notable (because in keeping with the national ethos) that the monastic movement which Llywelyn encouraged was that of the Cistercians, an order favouring austerity and self-provision, founding houses in remote and inaccessible places, by striking contrast to the comfortable Benedictines, who lived quite happily in the Norman castle towns and so quite easily became baronial allies. The Cistercians were acceptable too to the Welsh for their independent political attitude.

Just as his subjects were characterised by their mobility, so Llywelyn and his court were itinerant too. In his absence a common court administered justice and kept order in each commote, but higher cases awaited the arrival of the prince. Although he was the ultimate law-giver, he was advised by a formal council, consisting of specific officers.

Chief among Llywelyn's entourage was his 'distain' or seneschal, Ednyfed Fychan, a man who became a force in Wales in his own right and set up a dynasty in North Wales which to a large extent determined the future squirearchy. He became head of Llywelyn's court in about 1218, when he was present at the Treaty of Worcester. He is referred to as 'steward' when witnessing charters in 1225 and 1230. He survived his master to become lieutenant to his successor, David, dying in 1246.

Local officials formed the basis of the static court, the 'maer' or mayor of the commote being replaced in power during this time by a new officer, the 'rhaglaw' or lieutenant, the prince's representative. He was supported by the legal officer and by the steward of the 'llys', as the static court was known. There was some administration involved as the court had to be permanently provided for. Each llys in each commote was surrounded by demesne lands sufficient for its provision.

While all this stayed put, Llywelyn and the itinerant court moved from llys to llys. With him was his seneschal Ednyfed and also his chancellor, together with a small number of clerks. He was protected by the 'teulu', the familiar term for his household troops.

The courts were not far apart. From Trefriw to Conwy, Conwy to Aber, is about eight miles. To go from Aber to Llanfaes would involve crossing the Lafan Sands at low tide and crossing the narrowed strait by ferry, but the distance is about the same. That there were major courts both at Rhosyr and Aberffraw, a few miles apart in western Anglesey (as has now become clear from the recent work done by the Gwynedd Archeological Trust) perhaps indicates that they were not all in use at the same time. Since we know that Llywelyn occupied Aberffraw, and also that he issued a charter from Rhosyr in 1237, we must suppose that one of these clearly alternative sites was coming into use, the other going out, during his lifetime. Certainly most of the finds at Rhosyr indicate a slightly later date, the time of his successors David and the last Llywelyn. Courts at Caernarfon and Nefyn, on the Llŷn peninsula, completed this chain.

Aberffraw had always been one of the principal seats of the kings of Gwynedd. There is nothing to be seen of the court there now, only a barely distinguishable bank in a field. It was widely assumed until the substantial stone wall-bases were uncovered in the early 1990's at Rhosyr that the reason for the disappearance of all Llywelyn's courts was that they were made of wood. It is known, certainly, that the court at Aberffraw was intentionally demolished and its timbers taken to repair and complete Caernarfon castle in 1317.

We know of Llywelyn's involvement with the ancient seat of his ancestors at Aberffraw because he incorporated it in his title. Until the spring of 1230 he was known as 'Princeps Norwallie', the latter area meaning in fact Gwynedd. After that it became 'Princeps Aberffraw et dominus de Snowdon'. The reason for the change is only clear if we understand the background.

Aberffraw was recognised in law as the chief court of Gwynedd. Thus the lord of Aberffraw was the ruler of the whole of Gwynedd. But it meant more than this. Just as to be lord of Dinefwr, in South Wales, gave the Lord Rhys the status of overlord, so the style Prince of Aberffraw commanded the loyalty of all the North Wales leaders.

Although Llywelyn's courts were civil settlements and, in their often lightly built form, scarcely defendable, they were supported by a network of impressive stone-built and presumably permanently garrisoned castles. These lay at strategic points in relation to the courts and to the borders of the kingdom. Thus the ancient Gwynedd fortress at Deganwy, for instance, could send help if need be to the courts of Trefriw, Conwy and Aber. Its existence would also add security to the Prince's passage between those places.

Llywelyn's castle-building belongs mainly to the 1220's, following the political consolidation of his rule. The castles were built at strategic points, guarding the main valley approaches to the heartland of Gwynedd. That at Ewloe protects the entry to Gwynedd via the coastal plain; Cricieth and Deganwy bracket the kingdom's coast; Dolwyddelan and Dolbadarn overlook main passes into the mountains. Castell y Bere, further south, overlooks the entry to Gwynedd from that direction up the winding Dysynni valley.

Among these there is an interesting variation of style. Richard Avent, in his useful booklet *Castles of the Princes of Gwynedd*, brings out the point that castle-building was at the time undergoing an innovation. Until the turn of the 12th to 13th century keeps were square. Thus Dolwyddelan (where Llywelyn almost certainly replaced an earlier motte with the basis of the present edifice) has a square keep. A rounded form (it was becoming apparent) was easier to defend. Hence a transition takes place. The towers at Ewloe and Cricieth are of a D form, their rounded ends looking, now, remarkably like Edward I's later wall-towers. Then, towards the end of the 1220's or in the 1230's, he built Dolbadarn castle on the Nant Gwynant pass, and the tower is firmly round. Llywelyn has observed, it is thought, the stylistic changes taking place in the castles of his neighbours and relatives on the English border.

When King John died, on 19th October 1216, after a last, failed attempt to regain his lands on the Welsh border, it was something of a mixed blessing for Llywelyn. The new king, Henry III, was only nine years old, so that the politics of England was in the hands of his major barons. Many of Llywelyn's former allies sided against him with the new king, obliging Llywelyn to assert his authority. This he did so effectively that a peace was arranged. The English leaders favoured appeasement. In return for doing homage to the new king at Worcester, in 1218, Llywelyn was allowed to keep his conquered lands. During Henry's minority, and that of Gwenwynwyn's heirs, Llywelyn was to control the royal castles of Cardigan and Carmarthen and the lands formerly given to Gwenwynwyn, including Montgomery. Evidently the king's party recognised the need to secure Henry's vulnerable throne by enlisting Llywelyn's powerful support. There were, however, to be one or two more setbacks to the establishment of his status as an independent prince.

Principal among Llywelyn's continuing problems was a long-running contest with William Marshal, Earl of Pembroke, which came to a head in 1223, when the Earl arrived from Ireland with an army and took possession of the castles which the king had entrusted to Llywelyn. He moved fast, taking Llywelyn, apparently, by surprise. On Easter Monday he took Cardigan, a week after he had landed, and by the following Wednesday he was in Carmarthen. Both castles surrendered to him without a fight. Llywelyn sent his son Gruffudd with a large army to oppose the Earl, and the two forces met at a bloody but inconclusive confrontation at Carmarthen bridge. Gruffudd's army limped home to Gwynedd, defeated by lack of supplies.

Royal intervention only partially succeeded in putting an end to the unrest, and it was not until William Marshal's death in 1231 that Llywelyn regained his power over the South Wales castles. Henry III himself was having trouble at the time with his more powerful barons, those of the Welsh marches among them. He was also considerably hampered by lack of revenue. The English chronicle makes no bones about this. When 'Llywelyn, prince of Wales, then began to sally over the borders in his usual fashion to ravage the lands of the English barons' the king's advisers told him he was suffering an affront to his royal dignity, letting the 'despicable robbers' roam his lands with impunity. 'I have been informed by my treasurers,' he replied, 'that all the revenues of my exchequer are scarcely enough to provide me with the simplest food and clothes . . . So my poverty does not allow me to make expeditions for war.'

Consequently when in 1233 Llywelyn took advantage of this situation to form an alliance with the new earl of Pembroke, in his quarrel with the king, Henry's action was conciliatory. A two-year truce was arranged, on 21st June, 1234, at Middle in Shropshire, a place half-way between Ellesmere and Shrewsbury. In the course of the campaign which preceded this Llywelyn had taken a significant prisoner, William de Breos, who during the course of his captivity agreed to marry his daughter to Llywelyn's son David, offering the castle of Builth as dowery. Part of the peace treaty obliged Llywelyn to pay a fine of £2,000, and he matched this precisely with William's ransom.

The truce made at Middle allowed Llywelyn to keep his earlier conquests, but agreed that no further castle-building or restoring would take place on either side. Since, after its two-year span, it was to be renewed year by year it represented peace for the rest of Llywelyn's life. He was thus able to concentrate on stabilising his succession.

Behind the great prince's public face we glimpse from time to time a mind not always free of personal anguish. The matter of the succession is symptomatic, since it highlights the central role played in his private life by his wife Joan. His elder son Gruffudd, though born before his marriage and to a woman who figured little in his father's life, might have expected, in Welsh custom, to inherit. Llywelyn's relationship with him had been erratic, to say the least.

In 1221 father and son had fallen out over the latter's manner of governing Meirionnydd, the territory he had been allotted and from which he was then forcibly removed. By 1223 he had apparently been forgiven, since he led his father's army into South Wales. In 1228 he fell out of favour again, and was imprisoned (in the ancestral castle at Deganwy) for the next six years.

Llywelyn started early establishing David as his agreed heir. He got the approval of the English crown in 1220. The boy was, after all, the new king's nephew. In 1222 the pope's approval was sought and gained, and the disinheritance of Gruffudd officially declared. In 1226 the Welsh leaders, effectively Llywelyn's Parliament, gave their support. In 1229 David went to do homage to his uncle, Henry III. The marriage to Isabella de Breos was an important political alliance, and it duly took place in 1230.

That this marriage took place is indeed surprising, in view of the events which immediately preceded it, which also reveal the prince's deep attachment to his wife Joan and reveal to us a short but vivid glimpse of the pangs of anguish in his life.

The father of his daughter-in-law to be, William de Breos, had evidently not been entirely idle during his imprisonment. When he came to visit his former captor the year after his release, for the Easter of 1230, Llywelyn evidently suspected that something was up. There is no doubt from the chronicles that he actually found his guest in bed with his wife. He reacted with a violent fury which his family had seen before. Both were thrown into prison. A few days later William was hanged.

He was hanged in public in the daytime, eight hundred men being present. It was, Sir John Lloyd credibly surmises, an event which startled the whole English realm. 'The deed,' he says, 'finds its explanation in a cruel domestic crisis, which shook Llywelyn through and through. It was the outraged husband, not the astute politician, who hanged William de Breos.'

Llywelyn wrote to the widow saying that judgement had been given by his magnates, who were outraged by William's behaviour. But the letter expresses no regret, and it is plain that the prince could have chosen to overrule the judgement. He adds that he wishes the marriage to go ahead, and hopes that his friendship with the family will continue. It is, to us, an astonishing approach to the widow of someone you have just hanged, but it may be seen as magnanimous, since William was undoubtedly guilty of disloyalty, not to say extreme folly.

But what of Joan? It takes two, after all, to instigate an infidelity. It seems that the prince's love for her was great enough to overcome his bitterness. She stayed in prison for a year, but in 1231 she was released and became again Llywelyn's valued mediator with the English crown.

Llywelyn's personal feelings were to erupt again in 1237. Llywelyn and Joan were at his court at Aber when she died, court of the commote of Arllechwedd Uchaf, a favourite place of his. She died on 2nd February. He had the body taken across the Lafan Sands and ferried to Llanfaes, where he also had a court. There he had Bishop Hugh of St Asaph (the see of Bangor being at that time vacant) consecrate a burial ground. And

On his death Llywelyn was buried at the monastery of Aberconwy, from where his coffin was moved to Maenan. The stone base of the sarcophagus is all that remains, preserved in the Wynn chapel of Llanrwst church.

he set up there a house of Franciscans, thought to be the holiest of monks, whose task was for ever to pray for her soul.

This they did until the Dissolution of the Monasteries. There is nothing to be seen of their monastery at Llanfaes now; only a reference to it in the form of the name of a house remains, The Friars, which stands on part of the site. At the Dissolution the elaborately carved stone coffin which bore the Princess was rescued, and preserved for some centuries at Baron Hill, seat of the local landowning family. There after a bit people seem to have forgotten what it was, since it became a horse-trough. It was again rescued in 1808 and placed in the porch of Beaumaris church, where it still is.

In that same year or early the next one Llywelyn, in his mid-60's, suffered a slight stroke. There was no change of policy in Gwynedd, and Llywelyn remained its head, but from then on his son Dafydd took on the actual running of the country. Charters were issued in his name in February 1238 and around that time. In 1238 the Welsh leaders were called to an assembly at Strata Florida where they each swore allegiance to Dafydd as the heir. Dafydd immediately began to assert his power. He confiscated most of the territory held by his brother Gruffudd, confining him to the Llŷn peninsula. The next year, not satisfied with that, he imprisoned him and his son Owain in Cricieth castle. It was not until after his father's death, when he suffered a defeat at the hands of his uncle the king of England, that he was obliged to release them. The unfortunate Gruffudd then became an English hostage, being held in the Tower of London by the king, who threatened to assert Gruffudd's right to a share of Gwynedd (which he, however, would hold on his protégé's behalf). Gruffudd, true to his luck, spoilt all this by trying to escape. It is one of the less heroic details of history that the rope of sheets with which he was climbing out of the Tower was too weak. It broke, and he fell to his death, in March 1244. We do not forget, of course, that he was vindicated in posterity; it was his son, not Dafydd's, who became the last Prince of independent Wales.

When it became quite clear to them that Llywelyn was dying, his people hurried him to the Abbey of Aberconwy, where he was enrolled as a monk, and died, as had his uncle Cynan, wearing the simple robe of undyed wool which gave the 'white monks' their name, in the Abbey of Aberconwy, on 11th April 1240.

Fortunately he was more likely to dwell then on the peaceful times behind him than the troubled times to come. The last years of his reign had seen a flowering of culture and religion in Wales which represents something of a golden period. The two great monasteries to which he had given charters, Cymer and Aberconwy, seats of thought and learning, symbolise this. It was a time when great books were produced. The laws of Wales, known traditionally at the Laws of Hywel Dda, were adapted and revised, at the start of the 13th century. Poets wrote whose work still stands high in the canon of Welsh literature. The Peniarth manuscript, which bears the earliest known version of the four branches of the Mabinogion, can be traced to around 1225.

Llywelyn was buried where he died, at Aberconwy. When the monastery was moved from there by Edward I they took the coffin of their patron with them to their new home at Maenan. From there it was rescued again at the Dissolution of the Monasteries. Like that of his wife it disappeared for a time, and only the bottom half of the sarcophagus was rediscovered, and is now in the Wynn chapel of Llanrwst church. The coffin which must have been inside this was buried by the monks somewhere in secret, and we do not know the resting-place of the bones of this great leader, the spot of which the poet Einion wrote:

True lord of the land – how strange that today
He does not rule over Gwynedd!
Lord of nothing but the piled up stones of his tomb,
Of the seven-foot grave in which he lies.

Owain Glyndŵr

No fault, no hunger, no shame,
No thirst ever at Sycharth.

Iolo Goch, virtually Owain's court bard, was an old man when he wrote about Sycharth, and he died before that world was destroyed for ever. He remembered the good times. Through him we see the gentle, courtly society in which Owain grew up and reached his prime, when Edward III and then his grandson Richard II were on the throne of England, and Wales was at peace with its neighbour. Before the overthrow of Richard changed England's destiny; before Glyndŵr's revolt set fire to Wales.

In fact the interplay between the two countries promised, at that time, to be of benefit to them both. Owain himself grew up very much in the style of a feudal marcher lord. Himself of royal descent (the heir of the princes of Powys on his father's side and of the lords of Deheubarth, in South Wales, on his mother's) he was sent to serve his apprenticeship, as was the feudal custom, in the retinue of his local overlord the Earl of Arundel. Nothing illustrates the complexity of the situation better than the fact that the Arundels were the major landowning family in North Wales at that time, and on friendly terms with the noble, though relatively impoverished, lords of Glyndyfrdwy.

The interplay went both ways. Iolo Goch wrote (in Welsh still) in praise of Edward III. If you wanted war you had to go to France with the Black Prince, as many Welshmen did, and Iolo wrote happily about that as well, clearly with no rancour that a Plantagenet was Prince of Wales.

Owain ap Gruffudd Fychan was born in about 1359 at his father's estate in the Dee valley. It was from that, Glyndyfrdwy, 'the valley of the water of the Dee', that they took their title and, in a shortened form, Glyn Dŵr, he later took his surname. We have to remember that after the conquest of Wales by Edward I in the 1280's the royal titles of Powys and Deheubarth meant little, and in English terms Owain would be judged by his wealth. Compared to that of the Earl of Arundel this was minute. It was based on two agricultural estates near Corwen, of which Sycharth was the family's main seat. In Welsh terms, by contrast, this made him a respectable landowner, as did the memory of the power of his lineage make him a man of status. Through his mother he also had property in west Wales, near Cardigan. The fact that his family had kept their lands intact was due to their having adopted the English rather than the Welsh custom of inheritance. Because of the system of division between all the male heirs the lands of the great Welsh families had, by Owain's time, become fragmented. His remained relatively substantial because of the accident that his grandfather had married into a Norman family, the Lestranges, and as a result had adopted the Norman form of inheritance.

Owain was only about ten when his father died, but it must be said that we know nothing of his next few years. Somebody must have looked after him and his estates until he came of age. R.R. Davies' speculation that it was his future father-in-law Sir David Hanmer is no more than that. The fact that that would explain how he came to marry Sir David's daughter is not exactly a compelling argument. Our evidence is slight as well for the next step in his career, a spell as legal student at the Inns of court; it is simply mentioned by one chronicler, and all that can be said of it apart from that is that it was a conventional phase of education for a young nobleman at the time.

The tendency among scholars now is to play down the role of Owain's English education. It is not, it is felt, as a lawyer that he shines, but as a military leader. Emphasis may therefore quite rightly be put on his military training. And luckily we know quite a bit about that.

In the 1380's Richard II was engaged in a campaign of containment on the Scottish border. Owain, aged about twenty-five, was at Berwick-on-Tweed in 1384, no doubt providing his feudal dues, in a garrison commanded by a Flintshire veteran, Sir Geoffrey Sais. It is strange for us to think of this bunch of Welshmen on the Scottish border fighting for the English against the Scots, but such alignments are a feature of the time and will occur again in this story. One of the effects of this posting would have been to make the young soldier aware of the role played in British affairs by the Percy family, the Earls of Northumberland.

It is right, at least, to stress the time taken, in his early manhood, by involvement in war, since he went to Scotland with Richard's troops the next year, 1385. Two years later he joined the force raised by his neighbouring landowner, the Earl of Arundel, to launch an expedition into France. In doing so he placed himself firmly among the feudal barons of the English-Welsh border, and also in the personal retinue of one of the most powerful men in the kingdom. Arundel, though based at Chirk, was during those years prominent in the unrest which surrounded Richard at court. The king had insulted him personally some years earlier, and, in a truly remarkable display of his personal temperament, had struck him in the face in Westminster Abbey. The earl was one of the Lords Appellant who virtually took over the running of the country towards the end of 1387. Glyndŵr was thus already involved in the politics of the nation.

We may find it surprising that he should spend so much time away at war during these years, since in 1383 he had got married. He married Margaret Hanmer, daughter of Sir David Hanmer, a King's Bench judge and member of the king's council, a powerful landowner in North Wales and a man of high standing in the legal world in England.

Like his grandfather, Gruffudd, Owain had in effect married into a local Norman family, albeit one that had deep roots in the borderland of North Wales. The Hanmers had come with Edward I, and so had been settled in the area of west Shropshire for a hundred years. The little village of Hanmer, after which they took their name, lies some five miles north-east of Ellesmere, technically enclosed in Wales by a curious loop of the border, but in character firmly placed in the agricultural prosperity of the English marches.

It would be misleading to imply that the Hanmers were English. A hundred years or more of cross-breeding on the border had, as Owain's pedigree itself displays, produced a society which could validly be called Anglo-Welsh. David Hanmer, his new father-in-law, had married the daughter of a respected Welsh line, property-owners in the area of Chirk, displaying again, if we needed further evidence, that families of standing of whichever origin treated each other with friendly respect, in that area, then.

The irony of this background amalgamation will underly, in this story, the polarisation into us-versus-them which Owain's revolt forced on the people of Wales and the Welsh border. Although Sir David died in 1387, before any of the conflict started, the loyalty of his family to Owain's cause is striking. Sir David's three sons, Gruffudd, John and Philip, were from the start among his closest supporters.

On the death of his father-in-law in the summer of 1387 Owain came home from his military service to play his part in the settling of family affairs.

The Hanmers made him one of the trustees, evidence perhaps (though slight) that he had some training in law. He did not go to war

The fine round mound of a medieval motte forms the base of Owain's famous court at Sycharth.

The most conspicuous feature of the court at Sycharth was apparently its broad moat, still containing some water.

again, though the campaign in France went on without him. Although it is still twelve years to the deposition of the king, and thirteen to the sparking of the revolt, what we very probably see before us during all that time is a contented country squire, a cultured, benevolent, prosperous and much-liked family man, at home in the Dee and Tanat valleys which he loved, minding his business and managing his estates.

With this breathing-space at our disposal, it is time perhaps to pay him a visit. Few homes have ever been described in such loving detail as that in the poem, with which we started this chapter, by Iolo Goch: 'Llys Owain Glyndŵr Yn Sycharth': Owain Glyndŵr's court at Sycharth.

Iolo looked forward with eager anticipation to his trips to Sycharth, he tells us. It was a place where old men were respected and poets always welcome. It was a courteous home. Then he paints it for us in words.

The first thing you noticed on approaching was the moat, a beautiful ring of water within an embankment. It is wide, evidently, since in the next line it is termed a lake, the court forming an island within it: 'a bridge across the lake, and one gateway for a hundred loads'. The court is roofed with jointed arches, workmanship which Iolo compares with St Patrick's bell-tower (by which he may perhaps mean Westminster Abbey), with French effects, with the cloisters at Westminster, in the gracefulness of the joints. Symmetrical, gilded bands bind the corners, and arched rafters above link together like a knot. Nine alcove rooms form twice as many mansions, in this fine wooden house on the top of a green hill.

The house is further elevated by four majestic pillars, on top of each of which is a well-built loft. And in these, which are convivially interjoined, the travelling minstrels sleep. A fine tribal nest, these four bright lofts seem like eight. Each part of the court has a tiled roof, and a chimney which expels the smoke. Nine matching halls each have their own wardrobe, stocked like fine shops with beautiful goods, like a shop as well-filled as in Cheapside, London. (We cannot help noticing that Iolo peppers his poem with English references, and even a number of English words).

The effect is cruciform, like a church, well-rounded, or like chapels with fine glass windows, limewashed. Every part of it is full, every dwelling in the court; an orchard and a vineyard make up the white-court fort.

Near the court, and adding to its beauty, deer graze in another park. The master and national lord's rabbit-warren, his ploughs and horses are well-known. Fine meadows of grass and hay, corn growing in well-kept fields. An attractive mill on still water; the stone tower of his dovecot. A hollowed-out fishpond, where you must cast your net; the place where, without doubt, pike and salmon are common. His terrace where his birds dwell, peacocks and lively herons.

After this appraisal of the setting he then describes the household. There are servants with their particular jobs, taking care of the whole area; bringing the best beer from Shrewsbury; other drinks of various sorts; white bread and wine; meat and the fire in the kitchen. There are always poets gathered from many places. The best wife of wives, whom I thank for her mead and wine, daughter of a clear line of knights, noble, hospitable, of royal blood. And the pairs of children, a fine nest of rulers. There are no locks or bolts to be seen around his home; there is no need of a gate-keeper; there are gifts here for all. No fault, no hunger, no shame, no thirst ever at Sycharth. Probably the best of Welshmen owns this land, of Pywer's people. It is a strong, lean warrior who owns this most lovable of courts.

The poem is written in much-compressed imagery, partly dictated by the strict AA, BB verse-form, though with largely unaffected, unstylised vocabulary which gives an impression of spontaneity, of being spoken straight from the heart. Its somewhat dense style makes it in many ways a 'difficult' poem, very hard to translate into English prose, as no doubt my rendering above makes clear. What comes over in the Welsh is that the poem was made to be said aloud, the loose trochaic tetrameter form (dum-ti dum-ti dum-ti dum) and the firm couplet rhyme giving it an ease and flow which, for all their art, seem natural. This ability is not unique to Iolo: Welsh verse of the time has a virility about it which allows us to hear the author's voice as earnest and forthright; but it means that we believe that the poet was fond of Sycharth, because, for one thing, he tells us why. We end up loving Iolo for his patent love of Owain. We feel that this is not the sort of job you do, however skilled, just because you are getting paid.

When you come to Sycharth now, in its remote, even inaccessible little valley of a tributary of the Tanat, you are inevitably aware of being deep into intensely rural, farming country. You have come down so many winding, tall-hedged lanes, seen so many sheep and so little traffic, you cannot but be conscious that this is a land where little ever changes. It is hard to believe that through it once ran a vicious war.

Expecting the site of a moated manor, you will be surprised to find instead that of a Norman motte-and-bailey castle. Glyndŵr, with unintended symbolism, built his modern residence on a much older site. This area of the Welsh marches came under Norman occupation before the end of the eleventh century, and the castle here was probably one of the earliest to be built. It was thus an old site by the time that Iolo Goch knew it, in about 1390. It is hard to see why the early conquerors chose this spot. Although it has an outlook across the surrounding fields it is itself noticeably overlooked, by a tall escarpment now thickly wooded, only a matter of yards away. One must suppose that the occupants of the castle would have to occupy that as well. It would, we feel, have been better to build in open country.

This would not, of course, have worried Glyndŵr. We have it on Iolo's authority that he didn't need to lock his doors. There was no need for a gate-keeper at Sycharth. What Glyndŵr must have spotted in the site is its imposing approach, the elevated stance of the motte at the top of a rising field giving it an imposing, grand air, a site well-suited to a chieftain's status. Here he placed his very English moated grange.

The motte, flat-topped, is some twenty-five yards across, so the hall could not have been as extensive as Iolo implies. It is finely rounded, and most striking is the depth and width of the ditch (still water-logged) which formed the moat, and the fineness of its encircling bank. A number of well-proportioned trees have sown themselves along it, including one majestic specimen of oak of awe-inspiring perfection. Looking down one side one can see, under the wooded crag, a patch of water-meadow where the fish-pond was.

During the years 1962-3 Sycharth was archeologically excavated by Douglas Hague and Cynthia Warhurst, whose findings are reported in the 1966 volume of *Archeologia Cambrensis*.

They found under the turf evidence of two structures on the top of the motte, one being a hall near the plateau's centre, estimated to have been up to forty-three feet long. In addition there was a separate building, to the east of the hall, a mere nine foot wide. The archeologists found it likely that the main structure was indeed Owain Glyndŵr's hall as described by Iolo Goch, though its narrow span indicates that Iolo was exaggerating about the spacious aisles. The second building, though judged to be contemporary, was more of a puzzle to them. 'Its purpose is a matter for speculation; one possible use may have been a latrine as there was a high phosphate content in the soil of the ditch section immediately below this building.' John Davies comments, in one of those deft asides which make history worth reading, and writing: 'It is difficult to get nearer than this to the poets and their patrons, for the phosphate provides evidence of the consequences of the much-praised hospitality of the lord of Sycharth.' It is true that a lot of the time historians inevitably work from secondary sources. The high phosphate content in the ditch below this building is, as Davies perceived, a true primary source.

Denbigh, a Norman castle well within Wales, was one of the first such enclosures to fall to Glyndŵr.

The recovery of Glyndŵr's rebellion after its initial set back came with the taking of Conwy castle by the Tudur brothers.

Finds in the Sycharth excavation were a disappointment. The largest amount of pottery sherds seems to have been from the late fourteenth century, confirming the identification. The lack of anything from earlier periods indicates that a total renovation took place at Glyndŵr's time, of a possibly long-abandoned site.

In addition to Sycharth, which was clearly his main home, Owain had a hunting lodge at Glyndyfrdwy, the property from which he took his name. In both locations he had as neighbours powerful Norman lords, whose lands bordered his own. At Sycharth he would have been mainly conscious of the presence at Chirk of the powerful Earl of Arundel. Further north in the Dee valley he would have looked north again to the lands of the lord of Ruthin, a Norman town surprisingly deep within Wales.

Owain had known Reginald Grey for some time, in fact since his youth. They had both fought as young men in the retinue of the Earl of Arundel, in the French campaign of 1387. Although the family owned land mainly in eastern England, Reginald was a frequent visitor to his Welsh estates. Perhaps such opportunity to meet was also a chance to come to dislike each other. Perhaps their eventual antagonism arose from less personal, political allegiance.

Towards the end of Owain's period of peace something of major significance to British history happened in North Wales. It must be said that in relation to the business of the betrayal of Richard II Glyndŵr was in an ambiguous position. He had fought for Richard in Scotland, but he had also been in the personal retinue of one of Richard's most bitter enemies, at a time when the latter was part of a virtual regency. There is even some suggestion, in some sources, that he had served for a time as a squire to Henry Bolingbroke, Duke of Lancaster, the future Henry IV. Sir John Lloyd doubts this, which is only mentioned in one chronicle, on the sensible grounds that it is hard to see when he could have fitted this in. In any case whatever Owain's past alliances may have inclined him to in the conflict which followed, there is no doubt from subsequent events that he found Henry a grave disappointment and, along with many Welshmen, resented Richard's downfall.

You could not have been in North Wales in the late summer of 1399 without having some feeling of involvement in the traumatic events that were going on. Richard returned from Ireland on 25th July and made for the safety of Conwy. Bolingbroke reached Chester about the same time, 9th August. By 19th he had coaxed Richard out of Conwy. Treacherously ambushed near Colwyn Bay, the doomed king was taken under escort to Rhuddlan and then on to Flint, where Bolingbroke awaited him. It is a folk-tale, only, that Glyndŵr was in his retinue at this time, and was taken prisoner with him. He may have witnessed, and anyway cannot have been unaware of, the armed party with their royal prisoner riding along the north coast towards a change of king.

The connection is that it was towards the end of that same year that the events which lay behind the revolt appear to have started.

There are traditionally said to be two direct causes of the outbreak, both of them to do with the personality and position of Reginald Grey. The one recorded in the official Annals for the year concerns a piece of land. As Pennant interprets it, Grey took advantage of the deposition of Richard (presumably because he was a favourite of the new king's) to seize a piece of disputed land which Glyndŵr had recovered from him by course of law during the previous reign. It is true that Grey's lands bordered at two points with Owain's. According to this version of the cause of trouble Glyndŵr then sought a legal solution and laid a case before Parliament. Grey was not only a personal friend of the king but a member of his Council, so that justice was unlikely. The case was dismissed.

You do not, however, even in Wales, go to war over a piece of land. The second cause cited is reported by the chronicler of Evesham, normally regarded as well-placed to receive the current news. This says that Henry, at the start of his reign, launched an expedition against the Scots, and summoned Owain, along with other lords owing him feudal dues, to join it. The writ was entrusted to Grey, to deliver it to Owain in Wales, but out of malice he neglected to do so until it was too late for Owain to act on it, apparently only three days before the expedition was due to leave. Grey reported back to Henry that Glyndŵr had refused, and represented him as a traitor. This, if it were true, would imply a pre-existing quarrel, perhaps again to do with disputed land.

It must be said, with only these two slight stories to go on, that the immediate causes of the outbreak of revolt are insignificant. There is nothing in Owain's previous behaviour which would lead us to expect him to react in such a way to a purely personal antagonism. We must look for causes in the background climate of unrest, which was evidently such as would catch fire at the slightest spark. Whatever Owain's own ambiguous position may have been in relation to the change from Richard to Henry, there is some reason to suppose that the people of Wales felt some personal loyalty to Richard, and since rumours continued to persist that he was still alive may have felt an emotional commitment to the cause of restoring him to rule. There is some indication that the Greys were personally disliked in the area, so that they could easily become the focus of an upsurge of latent resentment.

The facts are agreed, about the next event, but the motive continues to baffle historians. On Thursday, 16th September, 1400, a group of relatives and neighbours gathered at Glyndyfrdwy, including his son Gruffudd, his brother Tudur, his wife's brothers Gruffudd and Philip Hanmer, his sister's husband Robert Puleston, the Dean of St Asaph with his two nephews, and some other friends and neighbours. There they proclaimed Owain Prince of Wales.

It is on the face of it an astonishing thing for him to have permitted to happen. R.R. Davies infers 'long-cherished dreams and aspirations'. The modern poet R.S. Thomas begins his poem in which Glyndŵr explains himself with the words 'Gruffudd Llwyd put into my head/The strange thought . . . ' and indeed Thomas Pennant, in trying to make sense of this sudden discovery of ambition quotes in full the relevant poem by Gruffudd Llwyd 'his chief bard'. Unlike the work of Iolo it is avowedly partisan and nationalistic. It compares Glyndŵr's position to that of Uther Pendragon, the father of King Arthur, and refers to 'good omens' which both leaders had in common. In this reference to Uther and to omens, and in the general theme of the Welsh fighting the Saxons, we see the clear influence of Geoffrey of Monmouth. Although the 'omen', in the form of a comet, did not appear (as we shall see) until 1402, and the poem probably dates from around then as well, I think there is a clue to be gained from the evident knowledge at Glyndŵr's court of Geoffrey's 'History', or (since the work was by then more than two hundred years old) some current adaptation of it. We shall find reason to suppose that Glyndŵr was affected at a later stage by an understanding of his national inheritance which he appears to have gained from Geoffrey; it might not be too fanciful to conclude from this that he could have been inspired at the outset too (as was his bard) by Geoffrey's heroic British nationalism.

The proclamation of Glyndŵr as Prince of Wales was an act of provocation at a national level, since there was already a rival Prince of Wales. The title, by which Llywelyn the Great was occasionally known and which had been held by official agreement with the English crown by Llywelyn the Last, had been annexed to the English monarchy by Edward I and thereafter bestowed on his eldest son, and the eldest sons of his successors. Accordingly one of the first things the new king, Henry IV, did, while Richard was still alive, on 15th October 1399, was to have the Earl of Arundel proclaim to Parliament that he proposed to create his son, the future Henry V, Prince of Wales. For Glyndŵr to claim the title less than a year later was tantamount to a denial of the legitimacy of

Henry's rule.

His first act however was distinctly local, and related to the personal aspect of his dispute. On the Saturday, 18th, he gathered a force at Glyndyfrdwy and they marched the ten miles north to Ruthin, Lord Grey's Norman borough within Wales, which they burnt. It was only a few days until the Ruthin fair of St Matthew's day, a major item, apparently, in the town's calendar, since the connection of the raid with the fair was remembered in local tradition. Encouraged by the success of this, and with gathering support, they went on during the next three days to destroy the other Norman towns within North Wales, the boroughs of Denbigh, Rhuddlan, Flint, Hawarden, and Holt, in the process reminding us how thorough had been Edward I's programme of networking his conquest with castle towns manned by his garrisons and burgesses. By the next Wednesday they had burnt Oswestry, and by the Thursday Welshpool. Then suddenly, on the Friday, the revolt came to an abrupt end, and that might well have been that.

Not far from Welshpool (perhaps intending to press on to Shrewsbury or Ludlow) they met, on the banks of the Severn, a contingent of English levies, the fighting men of Shropshire, Staffordshire and Warwickshire, under Hugh Burnell, a magnate of the Shrewsbury region. The Welsh rabble was ignominiously defeated. There were, at this stage, only a small number of them, perhaps less than three hundred. Some of them now simply went home, thinking this rumpus was over. Owain and his close associates took to the woods and hills.

This was on the 24th. The news had already reached Henry, at Northampton, on the 19th, as he made his way back from the Scottish campaign which, had things gone differently, Glyndŵr might well have attended himself. He took the matter seriously, sensitive evidently to the danger of all-out revolt in Wales. He turned westwards himself, while sending out orders to raise troops in ten counties. He sent a message to the border town of Shrewsbury, warning the citizens to beware of the town's resident Welsh. The king was in Coventry by the 22nd, Litchfield on the 23rd, and he reached the border at Shrewsbury on the 26th.

Meanwhile in Anglesey support for the rebellion had been expressed by the Tudur family of Penmynydd, ancestors of the future British monarchs and cousins of Glyndŵr's. It was perhaps for this reason that Henry marched as far as Bangor and Caernarfon, which he reached about 9th October. Rhys and Gwilym ap Tudur were, after all, still there, whereas Glyndŵr had disappeared.

With the royal army so far within Wales most of the population was happy to submit to the king. They were led in this by the church. The abbots of Cymer, Bardsey and Maenan sided with Henry, as did the rector of Llanllechid. Only the monastery of Llanfaes continued to support the rebels, for which indiscretion it was promptly gutted, and it remained thereafter derelict until Henry re-established it in January 1401. Evidently feeling he had delivered sufficient warning to the Tudurs Henry went back to Shrewsbury, which he reached on the 15th.

The missing leaders had become effectively outlaws. Some of the Hanmers themselves were dispossessed, as was Robert Puleston, and on 8th November all Owain's manors and lands were given to John Beaufort, Earl of Somerset. Those who remained at home, such as Owain's brother Tudur and the Dean of St Asaph, hastily submitted to the king.

Though the rebellion had, on the face of it, been a complete failure, there evidently remained undercurrents enough to cause concern in England, since the matter was raised when Parliament sat in January 1401, and a report was submitted to it on 21st February announcing that Wales was still unsettled. Indeed it was evidently much more unsettled than it appeared, since Welsh scholars at Oxford and Cambridge were leaving their desks and travelling homewards, and Welsh labourers working in England were leaving their jobs and going, as they seemed to think, to join the war. Parliament's reaction was to pass a Statute restricting the rights of the Welsh in England and instructing the Marcher lords to fortify their castles.

Meanwhile, although Henry himself had returned, he had left his son Prince Henry and the latter's friend Henry Percy, known as Hotspur, in Chester. Percy in fact now had the title of Justice of Chester and North Wales, making him the king's lieutenant in the area, and he had control as well of the Norman castles along the coast, being sheriff of Flint, holder of Anglesey and Beaumaris, and keeper of the lordship of Denbigh. His policy was appeasement; he pardoned widely. He drew the line, however, at pardoning Owain and his cousins the Tudurs.

One of the problems about telling Glyndŵr's story is that a lot of the action takes place with the hero offstage. For the time being he has completely disappeared. An outlaw, a wanted man, we may imagine him hiding in caves in the Berwyn hills, no longer Lord of Glyndyfrdwy or of anything at all, Prince of Wales only in the most ironic sense, having lost his patrimony and fallen far from the height of his hereditary status. Whatever it was that caused the scholars and labourers to trickle homewards during the early months of 1401, it does not seem likely to have been directly caused by Owain himself.

The next event in the incipient turmoil is also only indirectly due to

The walled town of Conwy was for a time in the hands of the rebels, in the early stages of the revolt.

Owain. The Tudur brothers were concerned with their own interests, specifically to gain a negotiating position from which to win their withheld pardon. This they achieved by a bravura exploit, worthy of the future destiny of their line.

With a company of only some forty men they took Conwy castle. Conwy castle has never fallen to storm – not even when bombarded through the summer and autumn of 1646 by the massed cannons of the Parliamentary army. It is, in terms of conventional warfare, impregnable, as indeed the Tudur brothers found, to their advantage, once they were inside. They took it by a simple but effective ruse of timing.

Good Friday in 1401 fell on April 1st. Because of the importance of that religious occasion they knew that at a certain time the garrison would be at service in the Parish church. Probably they and their men were in the town already, among the throng of country people who came within the walls during the day to trade. They forced their way into the castle, and once they were secure within it the people of the vicinity, seizing an opportunity, proceeded to devastate the town.

Caught wrong-footed the hapless Constable and Henry Percy were confronted with a dilemma. Conwy, both the castle and the town, were now in Welsh hands. Clearly, given the climate of the time, this was a state of affairs which could not continue. Percy, who had more reason than ever now to refuse them a pardon, was obliged to climb down. He started the process of doing so on 13th April, but the negociations were complicated by conflicting pressures. To allow these clearly dangerous men to get away with this could prove inflammatory. It was Conwy's impregnability which decided the issue. The Tudur brothers could wait as long as they chose. It was not until late in June that they found terms they could agree to. They handed over eight of their men to the English, but they themselves were free to go, and with the full pardon they had come to Conwy to obtain.

Suddenly and without warning Glyndŵr reappeared. It was to prove one of his most effective tactics, appearing unexpectedly with a band of men out of the hills. As R.R. Davies emphasises, it was, to begin with at any rate, essentially a guerrilla war.

A large English army had gathered in the Pumlumon area, on the banks of the river Hyddgen. No doubt the force was gathered there for the purpose of tracking him down and defeating him, but why then they were in Montgomeryshire remains a puzzle. Clearly they knew more than we did: they knew where he was. Clearly also they did not expect him to emerge when he did, since he defeated them soundly.

It was this defeat which sparked the second phase of the war. News was brought to Henry at Wallingford on 26th May, and it was perhaps what he had been waiting for. He summoned troops from fourteen counties to meet him at Worcester.

That would have been some three to four thousand men. Henry saw his task as wiping the rebellion out completely. He had in his possession a letter which Glyndŵr had written summoning the support of Henry Don of Kidwelly, in which the Welsh leader claimed to have been sent by God to liberate the Welsh from their captivity by the English. Support for Owain was growing in central and southern Wales, and he ruled almost all of North Wales as if by right. Nevertheless for some reason the June expedition was postponed, perhaps a crucial error on Henry's part. He appears to have thought the danger was now over, and to have dismissed his troops. He called them again, however, in September, realising his mistake. The Welsh rebels had spent the summer gathering support and causing havoc. Henry was back at Worcester in October, and this time he led his army into South Wales.

Although there was no sign of Glyndŵr himself there was it seems much show of support for him in South Wales, since Henry burnt much of it and carried out public executions, confiscating the property of all supposed dissidents. He even dealt severely with the monastery of Strata Florida, which he requisitioned as his headquarters. The short-term effect was no doubt to spread both unpopularity and fear; in the longer term Henry arranged for the royal castles in south and mid Wales to be put into a state of defence.

Henry Percy was away in Scotland that October when (with the king in the south) Glyndŵr attacked Welshpool, and seized the baggage train of the king's son, the Prince of Wales. On November 2nd the royal town of Caernarfon was threatened, evidently with a sizeable force, since on this occasion, in a set-back which must have demoralised the rebels, Owain lost some three hundred men. The event is significant for another reason. Adam of Usk (on whom we rely for our contemporary account of much of this) mentions that the standard Owain bore outside the town displayed a golden dragon on a white background. This indicates a detailed knowledge of Geoffrey of Monmouth (viii 17), who recounts that Uther Pendragon, the father of King Arthur, carried such a golden dragon as his standard when he went to war.

That autumn, of 1401, the king's Council considered peace. Sir John Lloyd comments: 'It was probably the one moment at which a peace satisfactory to both parties might have been concluded.' Nevertheless it did not take place. Instead we find Owain that November writing to ask support from the Irish chiefs and Robert III of Scotland. Neither letter got there; the messengers were intercepted. But Adam of Usk copied them in his chronicle, and it is interesting to see that in the letter to the king of Scotland (which he wrote in French) he claimed kinship through a common descent from Brutus, citing the geneology invented by Geoffrey of Monmouth, and referring to his own descent from Cadwaladr, 'the last crowned king of my nation'. In this indeed he seems to have assumed that Robert was familiar with Geoffrey of Monmouth as well, since the point about Cadwaladr is that, according to him, an angelic voice informed him that 'God did not wish the Britons to rule in Britain any more, until the moment should come which Merlin had prophesied to Arthur'. It is clear, in fact, that Glyndŵr's aspirations were becoming little short of messianic.

It is thought, and seems likely, that the abandonment of the considered negociations was due to the influence at court of the earl of Ruthin, Reginald Grey. This might explain why at the beginning of 1402 Glyndŵr attacked the lordship of Ruthin again and plundered the Clwyd valley. Adam of Usk points out that he avoided the adjoining lordship of Denbigh, which was the territory of Henry Percy, who now for the first time emerges as a potential supporter of the rebellion.

The year 1402 was to be a triumphant one for Owain, and in February and March a portent duly prefigured this. A comet blazed in the sky, which the Welsh bards heralded as the third great star of history. The first was the star of Bethlehem, of course. The second reveals the unwitting part played in these events by Geoffrey of Monmouth, since it was the comet which flared at the time of the succession as king of Britain of Uther Pendragon, said by Merlin to represent the greatness of Uther and his son King Arthur. The third which blazed so brightly over Anglesey betokened the long-awaited prophesied native revival.

Sure enough things at once started to go Glyndŵr's way. About the middle of April Reginald Grey himself was lured into a trap, near his castle of Ruthin, and became the rebels' captive. Henry Percy was back in Chester, and on 4th June he came to Denbigh in person with the task of relieving the now threatened coastal castles. By the middle of June, however, Owain was in north-east Radnorshire, which was Mortimer country. The young heir, then aged ten, was with the king, since he it was who was the rightful heir to the throne, the true successor to Richard II. Edward Mortimer had succeeded his brother Roger in 1398 and ruled over their lands on the Welsh border. He now raised troops in Hereford and mustered an army at Ludlow, from where he set out on 22nd June to confront the rebels. They met at Bryn Glas, a hill to the west of the village of Pilleth, near the river Lugg. The English troops had

Welsh archers with them, doubtless because these were feudal subjects of the Mortimers. It was crucial to the outcome of the Battle of Bryn Glas that these defected, turning their arrows on their former lords. The English were slain in large numbers and many of them captured. Among these was Mortimer himself.

Glyndŵr now had two of the major protagonists in this saga under his control, and much of the country on his side. When Henry was told of the slaughter three days later it must have chilled his heart. Never free of threats to his throne, he was at this time harassed by the French and by the Scots. He called a general muster at Litchfield on 7th July. Other enemies seemed at the time more pressing than the Welsh, however, and Owain was given a crucial space in which to consolidate his advantage.

By contrast to the band of guerrillas as which they had started out, Glyndŵr now had under his command an army of many thousands. How this was financed it is not clear, since his accounts, if any, have been lost; but it seems likely his attacks on church property, which took place in the early part of 1402, were motivated as much by the need for funds as by revenge for their support of the English and the usurpation. It was also a shrewd move to keep the captured Grey as an investment, rather than taking revenge by destroying him, since Glyndŵr knew, as would eventually prove to be so, that as a close friend of the king's he would command a substantial ransom. While he pillaged some monasteries, moreover, he was supported by others; the Franciscans, who had stayed loyal to Richard, collected funds for him.

Henry's discomfort was increased, that year, by the rumour that Richard II was alive and well and living in Wales. In the end he had no option but to attack. Owain had successfully expanded into South Wales during August, and at the end of that month the English armies moved. It was a three-pronged attack, from Chester, Shrewsbury and Hereford, the king taking the lead of the Shropshire wing, prince Henry that from Chester, and the earl of Stafford the third. Adam of Usk gives a figure of a hundred thousand men, but since he himself had gone to Rome in February he is going on hearsay at this point, and we have no certain figure.

Against this formidable and determined campaign the Welsh had their usual allies. The mountains helped them to disappear and avoid pitched battle. The weather now came to their aid as well. Knowing as we do the unpredictability of our climate it does not surprise us to hear of hail and snow in September, but for the English soldiers at the time it was a proof of Owain's powers of sorcery: he could command the forces of nature. It was the first occasion when a new aspect of him arose in people's minds, a supernatural dimension to a figure already endowed with the aura of mythic prophecy.

So bad was the storm that on one occasion (the night of 7th September) it, rather than the Welsh army, succeeded in threatening the king's life. His tent blew down around him, and only the fact that he was sleeping in his armour saved him from probably mortal injury.

The English were ill and exhausted as they returned, ignominiously, from Wales. In October Parliament passed, resentfully, a number of harsh anti-Welsh laws: they were deprived of the right of trying Englishmen in Wales; itinerant minstrels were prohibited from expressing pro-Welsh sentiments; gatherings were forbidden in Wales except under the control of the lord's officers; only those Welshmen who were fighting for the king might bear arms. Arms and supplies to Wales were banned, except for the use of the English garrisons. The Welsh were not allowed to fortify castles, to hold public office, to form part of the garrisons of the fortified towns, and even Englishmen married to Welsh women were forbidden to hold office in Wales or the Marches. All this was of course fairly ineffective while the Welsh remained defiant, and Parliament did not seem, that October, to know what to do.

In fact far from being able to impose their will on the Welsh, the government of England had to take account of the fact that Glyndŵr still held two significant bargaining assets: Mortimer and Grey. Both Henry and Parliament were particularly eager to rescue the latter. On 10th October a delegation of knights and gentlemen were sent to negotiate with Owain and his council – an indication that he was now a politically organised force. In the end he let Grey go for economic reasons: the ransom of 10,000 marks gave him a sound base from which to continue his campaign. At the same time it ruined Grey, whose finances never recovered.

Mortimer's usefulness shortly took a different form. He, unlike Grey, did not receive royal support. To Henry, the Mortimers were rivals for his throne. Thus it was that a situation was unwittingly set up in which this cause could become a factor in the war. By offering to help Mortimer in his claim Glyndŵr won his support. Mortimer, now a guest rather than a prisoner, changed sides. He sealed this alliance in the common, and effective, diplomatic way: by marriage. In November 1402 he married Glyndŵr's daughter Catherine. The programme of the Welsh revolt has now moved up a level: it is no longer just about restoring to Owain his lands; it is not even about the rights of the Welsh people. It is now nothing less than a movement to oust Henry from the throne.

If Richard is alive, Owain agreed with Mortimer, they would restore

*His failure to take the royal town of Caernarfon in 1401 was one
of Owain's first set-backs.*

*Harlech castle became a headquarters for Glyndŵr,
and was the last of his strongholds to fall.*

him to the throne. If he is dead the throne would go to Mortimer's nephew, the ultimate heir. This is a programme very much designed to appeal to the anti-Henry, pro-Richard faction throughout Britain. The immediate result of this was perhaps unexpected, but crucial to the next phase of the war.

Henry Percy, known as Hotspur, had been growing discontented with the king's behaviour. Edmund Mortimer, Glyndŵr's prisoner, was his wife's brother, and he cannot have failed to notice that Henry was far from eager to have him released. Having married into the Mortimer family he was in any case a natural ally of the Richard cause. Morover the Percy family and Glyndŵr had a relationship of mutual respect, learnt in the days when they campaigned together in the northern wars. It seems that discussions started in April 1403, and certainly by July the Percies were in open revolt in support of the Welsh.

In the meantime things had started to heat up. Prince Henry (who was now aged sixteen) was sent into North Wales, in a new role of royal deputy. He started his preparations in March, and in May led a triumphant raid into the enemy chieftain's home territory. From Shrewsbury on 15th May he wrote to his father to describe this action. He had come to Sycharth and found it empty. He burnt it to the ground. He then went on to 'Glyndourdy' (as the locals still pronounce Glyndyfrdwy) where he came to Glyndŵr's other dwelling, and he burnt his lodge there too and destroyed his park and laid waste the surrounding country. Many of Owain's followers were captured or killed.

The prince reports again to his father at the end of the month. His situation is not as sound as it might seem since his troops have not been paid and are ready to desert. The Welsh have been besieging the royal castles of Harlech and Aberystwyth for some time and if these are not relieved soon it will be too late.

Henry's hesitation once again gave Glyndŵr the chance to consolidate and advance. In June it was deemed necessary to defend the Marches, an invasion from Wales being expected. By 10th July Henry was heading back to the Scottish border, but he sent his son a thousand pounds to pay his troops, who were now getting dangerously restless. But it was the same day that Hotspur announced his change of allegiance.

We have to see his move in the immediate context of the Scottish wars, in which the house of Northumberland had, it seems, been thwarted in its rights of war by the king, inclining the earl, in fact, to side with the Scots; and in the longer context of the ambitions and traditional independence of the Percy family itself, which saw its role as being that of an almost autonomous buffer state. In general the further they were from London the stronger and freer were the feudal lords.

That July the whole of Wales was in patriotic revolt. Glyndŵr had an army of more than eight thousand men, and people flocked to join him wherever he marched. He took Carmarthen on Friday 6th, a blow to the royal side which spread panic in south and mid Wales. He moved on from there into the south-west, and was, as it happens, at Laugharne, on the next Tuesday, the day that Hotspur raised his standard at Chester.

The king on his way north heard of the defection on 13th July, at Nottingham, by which time large numbers of Cheshire and Welsh border people had joined Hotspur. Glyndŵr broke off his south-Wales campaign to march to join the Percy army, which was now heading for Shrewsbury. Henry, as so often before, turned abruptly west, summoned the forces of twelve counties, headed for Shrewsbury himself. He got there first, joining his son the Prince of Wales, who was already there. Glyndŵr had not arrived, and perhaps from his point of view this was just as well. His tactics would not have been suited to the pitched battle in open country which then followed.

Henry's swift and (for once) decisive movement had been intended to prevent the joining of rebel forces.

The next day, the 21st, was a Saturday. The rebel English army waited a few miles outside the town for the king and prince to come out. They had the smaller army, an uncertain figure reports of which ranged from nine to twenty thousand men. The royal army apparently had already moved, however, to take up a position advantageous to their number near Haughmond Abbey. During the morning the two approached each other and attempts were made to negotiate. The battle did not begin until late in the afternoon, when it lasted for two to three hours. Losses were heavy, and one of those who fell in the confusion of the mêlée was Hotspur himself. When they heard he was dead the rebels fled, and those who failed to escape were executed two days later. A chantry was raised on the site to commemorate the dead, and is now Battlefield church.

Speculation as to what would have happened had Glyndŵr been there could go either way, and so is not greatly helpful. If his presence had caused victory it would have been the end of the Lancastrian monarchy; if he had been a party to the defeat it would have been the end of the Welsh war. He was not there, and what might have seemed a major setback to his cause turned out to be only an incident in its progress.

Although Henry Percy had been killed his father, Northumberland, was still a powerful force in the north. This is the same man who four years earlier had been sent by Henry to lure King Richard out of Conwy.

He had lied on oath to achieve this. Henry had rewarded him for this; but inadequately, he felt, for his part in defending the Scottish border. He was a man not to be trifled with. In any case Henry had now killed his son.

The fruit of that was to come later, but at the time Owain's fortunes advanced with speed. Towards the end of that summer the border was ravaged by Welsh attacks, and there were assaults on Caernarfon and Kidwelly. Henry launched an expedition to try to recover South Wales. This seemed successful, as no-one resisted and most protested their loyalty, and it was not long before he was back in England. This was perhaps a misjudgement, since the Welsh rebels now had the aid of ships from France. If Henry thought the trouble would simply die down he was mistaken. Unrest was spread throughout Wales, and no royal castle was safe.

The next year, 1404, saw the culmination of Owain's success. While the French were pressing Caernarfon the main Welsh force had Harlech besieged, the garrison inside weakened by disease, and the castle fell in April. Shortly after Aberystwyth, also long besieged, fell too; and with these in this control Owain's status and authority was firmly established. It was now time to formalise his political aims.

Details of how he set about doing so have the air of folklore, but since Owain was quite clearly disposed to take up heroic, not to say romantic, positions, the truth may be as colourful as the legend. Adam of Usk tells us that he called a Parliament at Machynlleth, a town which lay in the middle of the area he now securely controlled. The 'Parliament House' which is the town's main pride today is thought by some authorities to be of a later date, but may represent the traditional site. It is reasonable to believe this, since it would be characteristic of Owain's understanding of his position as national leader that he should adopt the current form of government. It is tempting too to believe the rest of the tradition, and see the occasion as one of ceremonial magnificence, when (it is said) he was formally crowned Prince of Wales, in the presence of envoys from France, Scotland and Castile.

As Prince of Wales he now had both a foreign and domestic policy. We have to remember that Charles VI of France was the father-in-law of Richard II, whose widow Isabel had been returned to the safety of France on 31st July, 1401, leaving the way clear for the French to be openly hostile to the usurping English king. Two envoys bore a formal request for help to the French king from 'Owynus dei gratia princeps Wallie', using his title in a document for the first time, writing from Dolgellau on 10th May, 1404.

His proposal of an alliance with the French and his request for arms and assistance met with a favourable response at the French court, and by July a treaty had been formed.

While this was going on the Welsh continued to attack the border country, which received inadequate help from the crown. A French fleet was on its way to help, sixty ships setting out from Brittany and Normandy in August with seven hundred men, and it must have seemed to Henry that his time was up. Yet this turned out to be more of a threat than an action, since the fleet sailed up and down the channel until the autumn, and in November, without having landed, and indeed without having gone anywhere near Wales, they went home. This strange episode has never been properly explained, and it seems that there must have been some communication which we do not know about passing between the French and the English kings.

Although this disappointment obstructed Glyndŵr's ultimate aim, that of ousting Henry, it left him securely in control of most of Wales, ruling his land from his court at Harlech castle, where he and his family sat in honoured state.

Now it was time to turn his attention to his political agenda. It was now, at the start of 1405, that he began to negotiate with the two other most powerful people in the realm. Both Northumberland and Mortimer had reason to wish to secure their position, knowing how Henry would have liked to be rid of them. The former at least was powerful and cunning, while Mortimer remained conscious of his family's right to the throne. While doubt hovers meanly over the accuracy of the recorded terms of the 'Tripartite Indenture', we may say that it certainly took place, being signed at the end of February 1405 in the house of the Archdeacon of Bangor.

Shakespeare got the scene from Holinshed who got it from Hall's chronicle, in which the event is mistakenly said to have taken place before the battle of Shrewsbury, with the result that Shakespeare has Hotspur, rather than his father, as one of the parties to the agreement. It must be said, if honesty is to win against romance, that the three great leaders were not in any case personally present at this historic event; the contract was sealed by their deputies. The details had been hammered out by intermediaries. They are, to historians, much as Shakespeare summarised them. Britain is to be carved up into three parts. The division assumes blithely that the Lancastrian monarchy has become an irrelevance.

Mortimer is to take the south, Northumberland the north, Glyndŵr the west. The exact delimitations of these parts show Mortimer to have been the weakest party, since although he would presumably be king of England, England now was to be what was left over, after Northumberland and Glyndŵr had carved up the rest. The Thames valley and East Anglia (apart from Norfolk) and the south coast were to be Mortimer's. Northumberland's share did not stop (as is sometimes said) at the Trent, but included Leicester, Northampton, Warwick and Norfolk. It is Glyndŵr's very precisely defined kingdom which is of interest. It included most of what was once Mercia, the fertile Cheshire and Shropshire plains which Wales had always coveted, and the rich valleys of Hereford. 'Since the days of Cadwallon of Gwynedd,' comments Sir John Lloyd, 'no Welsh prince had presumed to claim so large an area of England . . . '

Rivers largely define its extent. Its border runs 'along the Severn to the North Gate of the city of Worcester, thence to the ash trees on the main road from Bridgnorth to Kinver: thence by the high way, called the ancient way, to the source of the Trent, then to the source of the Mersey, and so along that river to the sea.'

The success of this grand scheme depended upon a number of factors, all of which, during that same year of 1405, ended in failure. It depended on the successful assertion by the Percy family of their power. In what seems to have been a separate movement the north of England rose in arms, at the instigation of Archbishop Scrope, of York. He had been allied with the Percy faction at the battle of Shrewsbury, and although he had since then kept his options open we may see this as basically a Northumberland challenge to the crown. Henry diverted his attention from South Wales, which he was preparing to attack, and hastily marched north. While this temporarily relieved Glyndŵr it had the desired effect on the northern rebellion, which was put down with surprising ease. Northumberland had to flee to Scotland. This was, to put it mildly, a setback to the grand scheme.

A second failure that year was a plot to kidnap the Mortimer heir from his state of royal custody at Windsor, and bring him to Wales, with the expectation of starting an English uprising against Henry. The wild scheme nearly came off, but the fleeing party was seized before it could reach Wales.

In the meantime things had certainly not been going well for the Welsh at home. In March they suffered a defeat in the Monnow valley, in South Wales, and Glyndŵr's eldest son, Gruffudd, was defeated and taken prisoner at Usk in May. He was taken to the Tower of London and died after a further six years of imprisonment of the plague. In the same battle Owain's brother Tudur died, and a legend says that for a moment the crowd thought it was the chief himself. It could be the close resemblance of Tudur to his brother which gave rise to the uncomfortable feeling which developed among the English troops that Glyndŵr, through magic, was able to be in different places at the same time.

In June an English army sailed from Dublin and attacked Anglesey, as ever the heartland of the revolt. Such was their success that the Welsh abandoned it and took to the mountains of Snowdonia.

One thing that the Tripartite Indenture almost certainly depended on was the support of the French. The document specifically mentions 'the oath of allegiance sworn by Glyndŵr to the king of France'. Now at last, in early August of that same fateful year, 1405, the French landed. A force totalling two thousand six hundred men landed at Milford Haven, where it is said Glyndŵr himself met them with an army of more than ten thousand men.

This combined force did well to start with, taking the town of Haverfordwest, moving on to Tenby, and a few days later taking (once again) Carmarthen.

Glyndŵr also gained control of Cardigan and the Teifi valley, and so was secure in the west. They turned their attention to the east and the English border. By the end of August they had passed through Hereford successfully and were on the outskirts of Worcester. There, at Woodbury Hill, they dug themselves in and waited for Henry.

Worcester was, of course, the limit to the country which Glyndŵr had claimed for himself as lord of western Britain. He had no ambitions beyond that. Taking England from the Lancastrian crown was, in terms of the Tripartite Indenture, Mortimer's problem. Nevertheless it would have helped his cause if he and his French allies had defeated the king at this point, and the battle they waited for is, reasonably, described by Sir John Lloyd as 'the decisive moment . . . in the duel between Owen and the king.'

Henry had been gathering troops since he first heard of the French landings. He was at Leicester by 19th August and arrived in Worcester three days later with an army about the same size as the combined one awaiting him.

The two confronted each other with neither being willing to risk an offensive. Skirmishes and maintained defences went on for a week, by the end of which Owain began to feel his weakness. He was happier in the secure base of his heartland; he was happier if necessary in the hills. Here well within enemy country he was unsure of his supply lines, and without that essential could not be sure of holding together so many men. When on campaign he had always been anxious to protect his line of retreat, and he pulled back now, before it was too late.

What had in effect caused the failure of the French expedition was the lack of support they encountered in the border counties. If Hereford and Worcester had been with them their supplies would have been secure. As it was more and more people flocked to the side of the king. A muster took place in Hereford on 29th August, and while the French and Welsh were secure within Wales Henry decided that further action was necessary. In September he marched again into Wales. It must have seemed to him and his troops like something more than coincidence that once again, as in a previous September, he was attacked by the weather rather than by the Welsh. A violent storm produced flash floods in the rivers of Glamorgan and in the confusion he lost his baggage train. Some forty wagons fell into the hands of the Welsh. Unable to proceed without the provisions they carried he retreated with loss of dignity to Hereford.

Some of the French, not wanting to spend winter in Wales, went home in November. A lot, however, remained. Undoubtedly their presence helped to keep the Welsh respectful to Owain's cause. It had not, however, proved sufficient to put into place the programme of the Tripartite Indenture. It was when they finally left in Lent next year that Glyndŵr's hold on the country began to weaken.

The French left because they could not see their aim, of invading England, ever coming about. When they came they did not have in mind a long-running internal skirmish between the Welsh and the English castles within Wales. But Glyndŵr was still firstly concerned with the bringing into being of an independent principality. He did not himself want to become king of England; he was happy to leave that to someone else. He wanted only to be a free prince of a free Wales. Meanwhile however Wales was damaged and impoverished in the attempt. Little or no help had in the end emerged from dissidents in England. Northumberland himself was a refugee, fleeing now from Scotland to Wales. A second French force sent to help the Welsh rebels fell largely into English hands, only a few ships reaching Wales. They do not seem to have helped much, since we now hear of little success. In October, 1406, Charles VI decided he could help no more. He had expected his efforts to be accompanied by a rising within England. After all his own part in the campaign was on the behalf of his widowed daughter. At the same time Scotland was prevented from taking part by the fact that its young king was an English hostage. Meanwhile the Welsh started to lose battles, and another of Owain's sons was killed. Prince Henry, nineteen now, had taken charge of the war, and he soon showed his military skill

Owain Glyndŵr held a Parliament at Machynlleth,
where the present 'Institute', known as Parliament House,
may be a later building on the same site.

It was from Dolgellau that Glyndŵr wrote,
as Prince of Wales, to the King of France.

of forceful leadership. Whereas his father had given the impression of lurching from crisis to crisis, and always making decisions too late, the future victor of Agincourt took the war to the enemy. He was given a free hand, and had only this task to concentrate on.

As the edges of Glyndŵr's principality crumbled it was really only his own strong personality that kept the war going, beyond the middle of 1406 when it might have abruptly ended. Region after region of Wales submitted to the English. By the end of the year even Anglesey had gone. Harlech, where he held his court, and Aberystwyth (against which Prince Henry now launched a determined attack) were about all the strength that remained in Glyndŵr's hands. This is now the summer of 1407, and the young prince draws up outside its walls his siege engines and the flower of his army. Once more Glyndŵr appears to have astounding luck. Disagreement arose in the English camp, and some of Henry's men, regarding the enterprise as hopeless, deserted, obliging the prince to call a truce. It was assumed that the castle would then surrender, but when Glyndŵr himself appeared to defend it the English prince gave up and withdrew much, if not all, of his force.

It was a bitter winter. Northumberland died in the snow of the Yorkshire moors in February. A truce with France had specifically excluded Glyndŵr, now that the anti-English cause there had been weakened by internal conflicts. By the end of that winter of 1407-8 he had no friends to turn to, and little power even in Wales other than that afforded by the two castles of Aberystwyth and Harlech. In the summer the Prince of Wales returned to the former. By 23rd September it had fallen. Glyndŵr was now virtually trapped in Harlech. This too was subject to a long and intense siege.

The Welsh fought back, however, against the besieging force, and Harlech proved hard to take. It did not fall until March the next year, when the castle surrendered. Many had died in the siege, including Glyndŵr's son-in-law Edmund Mortimer. When the English entered the castle they took possession of all his goods and of his family too. His wife, two of his daughters, including Mortimer's widow Catherine, and the three Mortimer grandchildren. Yet he himself escaped; once again when they looked for him he was not there. Along with his only surviving son, Maredudd, he disappeared.

The scant clues as to his movements then seem to indicate that he went back to the area of Chirk, since lordships in the surrounding area were accused of negotiating with him. He clearly had a band of supporters still, including some he had started with, the Bishop of St Asaph, Philip Hanmer, two of the Tudurs.

One last foray, in 1410, marks the end of this dying phase of his career. He launched a raid on the Shropshire border, which was effectively repulsed by the constable of Welshpool. Three of his leading supporters were captured and in due course executed as traitors. Among them was Rhys ap Tudur of Penmynydd, his cousin, who, long ago as it seemed, had led the small band which successfully took Conwy castle in 1401. He met his judicial fate in Chester in that year, 1410.

Only rumour and inference followed Owain then until 1413, and then not even that.

In 1413 Henry IV was succeeded by his son. On his way to his successes in the French wars he sought to heal old wounds at home. In July 1415 he offered Owain a pardon. There was no response, but he tried again in February of the next year. This time the offer was made through Owain's son, Maredudd, and the fact that the next offer of a pardon was to Maredudd on his own is one possible clue that at least by that time, in April 1417, Owain Glyndŵr was known to be dead.

The time, place and manner of his death are not known. It is possible (following Sir John Lloyd) that he went into peaceful retirement at the home of his daughter Alice Scudamore, whose husband John had a manor at Monnington in Herefordshire, in the Golden Valley. The complete lack of evidence makes his death of legendary quality, like his life. 'Many say that he died,' one old source states; 'the poets say that he did not.'

In a poetic sense, of course, it is true. The rising of his spirit again will come with a renewal of Wales' pride. Some feel it is a long time coming. 'It is winter still in the bare tree,' wrote the poet R.S. Thomas:

But here at its roots I watch and wait
For the new spring so long delayed.

Of the many folk stories told of Glyndŵr, which (since this is history) I have not included here, one neatly sums up the ultimate cause of the failure of the Welsh rebellion: the time was not yet right. In a sense the seeds then sown were not to fruit until the establishment of the Tudor monarchy, the descendants of the Anglesey family who had supported their cousin throughout the war – when, at last, Wales could cease to feel a conquered nation and take an equal part in Britain's political business.

One daybreak in the Berwyn hills Glyndŵr encounters the Abbot of Valle Crucis, and remarks in surprise: 'You have risen early, Father.' 'No,' says the Abbot sadly, 'it is you who have risen early, by a hundred years.'

Sir John Wynn

I am looking at a man with a slightly florid face, whose expensive clothes proclaim, rather than mask, the rotundity of good living. It is a noticeably pleasant face, large attentive eyes showing the hint of a smile, the effect perhaps helped by a silken Father-Christmas beard. His hat is pushed back slightly to let the light fall on it and his open gaze fall on us. Plump hands, silk-cuffed, rest on a sword and the arm of the chair. A high, clearly fashionable, ruff, stands out, caught in the light, against his dark garments and the dark green wall behind him.

This is Sir John at his prime, in the Gwydir portrait, even the near-identical one at Mostyn Hall showing some of the erosions of physiognomy which age, worry and illness were to make so poignant a feature of the later portraits. He was a tall man, dark-haired in his youth, silver-bearded in the portraits, a large man whose presence, the portraits make clear, would always have been noticeable.

> The country people have a tradition, that he was a great oppressor; and accordingly have sent his perturbed spirit to reside in the neighbouring cataract of Rhaeadr y Wennol.

So reports Pennant; and no doubt you cannot rise to a position of such great power without exerting a firm hand. Much of Wynn's time was taken up in litigation with his tenants and his neighbours, in what seems to have been a constant struggle to keep his grip on his family's vast estates.

It was by a combination of historical and personal factors that they came by these, and he by his position at the culmination of the family's success, and hence the power and influence which he exerted over the whole of North Wales at a pivotal historical moment. He himself is keen that we should know where he comes from, believing that 'a great temporall blessinge yt is, and a great harts ease to a man to finde that he is well dissended'; and a large part of the motive of his book, 'The History of the Gwydir Family' is to convince us that he is no upstart.

Sir John in fact traces his ancestry back to Gruffudd ap Cynan, the twelfth century father of Owain Gwynedd and hence great-grandfather of Llywelyn the Great. If this lineage were correct it would have the remarkable result that in this book so far we have dealt with a thousand years of the history of North Wales in terms of the leadership exerted by the members of a single family. Lineage, as we have seen before, was of special importance to the people of Wales largely because it was embodied in their law, and Sir John's preoccupation with his pedigree was not just a means of legitimising his position of supremacy but a compliance, totally in keeping with his attitudes, with a strong cultural tradition.

Whether Sir John could confidently trace his ancestry back to the early princes is open to question, and some historians doubt it, but it is certain that his family tradition recorded accurately the migration of his great-grandfather and his family from their homelands of Eifionydd into the Dolwyddelan valley in around the year 1485. That year was, of course, a significant one in British history and something of a turning-point as well in Wales, since it formed the start of the Tudor monarchy. Sir John is of particular interest to us because he was a product of the changes directly brought about by this, so that his career, indeed his very occurrence, provide us with a valuable insight into the way modern Wales came into being.

When Maredudd ap Ieuan moved from Eifionydd to Dolwyddelan he did so in the aftermath of a period of lawlessness rather than with any consciousness of heralding the start of a new age. Sir John quotes his ancestor's reply to those who asked the reason for his move: he would, he said, rather fight with outlaws and thieves than with his own blood and kindred: 'for if I live in my house in Eifionydd I must either kill my own kinsmen or be killed by them'. The choice, however, was a stark one. In the final years of the Wars of the Roses the upper reaches of the Conwy and Lledr valleys were wild and lawless places. They were, for one thing, densely wooded, and Maredudd lived there in constant fear of being ambushed. This was comparatively normal, but there was in that area a particular cause of trouble, 'a wasp's nest,' says Sir John, 'which troubled the whole country'.

This was a hospice of the knights of St John founded at Ysbyty Ifan (so called for that reason) about the year 1189. It provided a safe refuge for travellers, including probably the stream of pilgrims heading for the holy island of Bardsey. However this role of sanctuary eventually became inverted, the hospice itself forming the sort of danger it was founded to protect people from. Because it was run by knights it had from the start immunities from state or royal interference. This meant that thieves and murderers were safe there too, and consequently it became a base for outlaws. No place within twenty miles, says Sir John, was safe from their incursions and robbery. It was largely because of this that the commote of Nanconwy, into which Maredudd was moving, was uninhabited wasteland.

It is significant to the subsequent story of the Wynn family that their ancestor moved into a largely vacant country. There were other, more general, historical reasons for this situation, besides the outlaws. Sir John, in his history of his family, places the blame firmly with Owain Glyndŵr. Eighty years later the country had not recovered from the devastation of his wars. North Wales was 'waste of inhabitants and all overgrown with woods,'

> for Owain Glyndŵr's wars, beginning in Anno 1400, continued fifteen years, which brought such a desolation that green grass grew on the market-place in Llanrwst called Bryn-y-boten and the deer fed in the churchyard of Llanrwst, as it is reported, for it was Owain Glyndŵr's policy to bring all things to waste, that the English should find not strength nor resting-place in the country. The country, being brought to such desolation, could not be replanted in haste . . .

Historians are less inclined now to attribute the undoubted period of stagnation in Wales in the years after Glyndŵr's revolt to his own policy of earth-scorching rather than to the depopulation caused by plague and to the political disorder, and demands on scant resources, caused by the long turmoil of the Wars of the Roses. When Maredudd moved at the very end of this period the country into which he came had a large number of vacant 'vills'. This land unit, developed from the Roman villa via the Saxon concept of a township, had become part of the feudal system in the form of the manor. The land was farmed by peasants on behalf of the lord. Depopulation made it impossible to sustain this system, and possible for men as enterprising as Maredudd to occupy such vills as had lost not only their tenants but their landlords too as a result.

That Maredudd was something of a formidable force seems certain from the results, as he acquired increasing areas of upland pasture and subsequently valley land at Llanrwst and Trefriw. The fact that he appears in his brass memorial in Dolwyddelan church in full military gear is significant. He probably wore it most of the time. The bard Tudur Aled aptly sums up the two aspects of his career: his acquisition of land and his force of arms.

*Sir John's portraits show a tall, slightly corpulent,
well-dressed man with a pleasant face.*

In all forms you grew
Giving your thick gold to buy land . . .
Your spear is broken fire, Maredudd,
Your blade, that must flow crimson.

Certainly what Sir John tells us of the way of life of his great-grandfather indicates that the acquisition of great estates was bought at the cost of constant fear. Even going to church on a Sunday was like a military engagement. He left his house bolted and defended. He had a lookout on a rock between the house and church. He travelled to church surrounded by twenty tall archers, and he never let it be known when he was going or went by the same route.

When Maredudd first came to Dolwyddelan he occupied the castle, which until recently had been the seat of an outlaw. It was only partly habitable and seems not to have been sufficiently spacious for Maredudd's growing family, since after some years he built himself a house in Cwm Penamnen. His personal family complexity may account for this, since he had a total of at least twenty children: ten by his first wife, two by his second. three by a third woman and another six by casual affairs. With at least some of this entourage he moved to live in 'the principal best ground in Dolwyddelan'.

Cwm Penamnen is a narrow steep-sided valley, very much (now) in a private world. The Roman road runs straight through it, however, and a Norman motte at its head indicates that it was once something of a thoroughfare. Old walls in the trees of the modern plantations give evidence of its former use, and there beside the road (in fact apparently either side of it) are the substantial ruins of Maredudd's homestead. A weir, now broken, constrained the river Penamnen, down to which Maredudd's house walls appear to have reached. Right opposite rears the pale-grey precipice of Carreg Altrem, and beyond the uplands stretch in open moorland towards the Machno valley.

We can see this founder of the Wynn family now in a surprisingly intimate portrait, in the form of a brass engraving in Dolwyddelan church. This church he himself had built, demolishing the former one which he found unsafe, through being in a thicket. It did not occur to him, apparently, to cut down the thicket; but perhaps a stronger motive for the move was that from his pew in the new church he could see his look-out on the high rock to the south-east, from where the look-out could see his house in Cwm Penamnen. If the latter were attacked Maredudd could rise from his devotions and go to its defence. In view of this it is appealing to find him, in this small and very finely worked brass plate, on his knees in full armour, his hands in prayer but his sword hanging by his side, his eyes alert and watchful, looking up and sideways, every bit as though attentive to a watchman on a rock.

Having thus established himself on good land in the Lledr valley Maredudd set about expanding. Once he had contained the banditry to his east he started acquiring possessions to the north, in the area of Trefriw and Llanrwst. Here towards the end of his life he built the first house at Gwydir. Sir John mentions him being there, on an occasion when he attended 'gymnastic games' at Llanrwst. He died, possibly at his new house, in 1525, at the age of sixty-five, and was (as we have seen from the brass memorial) buried at Dolwyddelan, his main territory. His son by his first marriage, John Wyn, succeeded him, inheriting the now vast properties in Eifionydd, the Lledr and Conwy valleys.

A number of historical events significant for the emerging Wynn family occurred during this period. John Wyn at Gwydir was well placed to take advantage of these, and on the Dissolution of the Monasteries in 1536 he acquired (as tenant to the Crown) a large amount of land, and it is likely that at least some materials from the demolished abbey at Maenan went to the making of his expanding mansion of Gwydir. It was the other great change of that year, as far as Wales was concerned, the Act of Union (as it later came to be called) which had the effect of permitting Welshmen to take up official office. It is rather surprising to us to find this taking place so late; and indeed people such as John Wyn and his father had held posts in ecclesiastical administration for some time. Now, from February 1536, the principle was initiated that the king's secular administration in Wales could be run by the Welsh as well.

The historian John Davies points out that the title 'Act of Union', which was not used for the statutes of 1536 until 1901, is misleading, firstly because it was a unilateral decision, Wales (unlike Scotland and Ireland at later dates) having no representation in Parliament; secondly because England and Wales were already legally united by the Statute of Rhuddlan. Essentially the 1536 legislation expanded and adjusted the earlier system.

Since the beginning of Tudor times the administration of local government in England had been in the hands of Justices of the Peace. In February 1536 this system was extended to much of Wales, and to the whole of it a few weeks later. This in effect meant that local landowners could become their county's administrative officers; and needless to say at once they did. Thus John Wyn in his time served as Member of Parliament, sheriff and Justice of the Peace. By doing so he set a pattern which was to be very much a characteristic of his family.

There is something of an inevitable momentum set up by the

combination of power and wealth. John Wyn ap Maredudd not only built for himself the grand country seat which Gwydir became, but he entered vigorously into the land market, employing an agent based in London to keep an eye on property values in North Wales. Although to a large extent his policy was one of consolidation, being mainly centred on Gwydir itself, it was also partly one of expansion, involving properties in the Ffestiniog valley and the Llŷn peninsula.

Some of this vast estate was made over in trust to his eldest son Morus before his death. When he died in 1559, aged sixty-six, Morus also received Gwydir and other lands at Trefriw, and some outlying properties not already settled on him, the rest being divided between the other two sons. Although the English legal system was now officially applicable to Wales, the custom of primogeniture, by which the eldest son gets the lot, had not yet been adopted. Still, for the time being, the Welsh gentry practised an element of gavelkind, the division of property between all the offspring, which Sir John, who was very much an empire-builder, referred to as 'the destruction of Wales', since it caused property to be 'mangled with division and subdivision'. The Wynns were always a large family, and their property was of a communal sort, held between many relatives. Nevertheless, following the Act of 'Union' primogeniture was creeping in; and it must be said that Morus Wynn inherited the lion's share.

Morus was the first of the family to adopt the surname Wynn, Henry VIII himself having recommended the Welsh gentry to adopt hereditary names. It had become the custom in England by the 1530's, when Parish records became compulsory. In spite of the adoption of the English legal system in Wales in 1536 the patronym continued to be used by non-landowning families for another two hundred years, as it did in highland Scotland. Morus Wynn however was, characteristically, being up to date. The name may well have been applied as a nickname to his grandfather Maredudd, perhaps referring to his fair complexion. The difference with adopting it as a surname is that it was now born by all members of the family.

The 1536 Act was largely the work of Thomas Cromwell, Henry VIII's chief administrator, who, however, fell foul of the king's notorious wilfulness and was executed in 1540. The Act had flaws, which were remedied piecemeal during the next few years and the results collected in a summarising Act of 1543. This underlined the intentions of the previous Act, making the legal and local government systems the same in Wales as in England, abolishing any restriction on Welsh trade (and thus allowing Welsh merchants to trade in England) and, significantly for the

Wynns, banning the old system of 'cyfran', or partible succession, the 'gavelkind' which Sir John blamed for Wales' weakness, and substituting the English system of primogeniture. This (as we have just observed) was not to take immediate or total effect.

Morus, like his father, spent his life consolidating his estates, and a valuable feature which he added to the family's fortunes was the alliance by marriage to great neighbouring landowners. In fact he did this three times, but the first is of greatest significance to our story, since it was to Jane, daughter of Sir Richard Bulkeley, head of the richest and most eminent family in North Wales at the time. It is not surprising that his son John, born at Gwydir in 1553, was to become so powerful and influential.

When we first hear from the man himself he is in London, aged nineteen, a law student at Furnival's Inn and about to be admitted to the Temple. Considerate correspondence between father and son at Gwydir and London continues, regarding both John's education, his marriage prospects, and the business of land in North Wales. Law suits too engage their attention, and there is the constant worry of the expense of keeping John in London. John for his part protests that he lives frugally, and that his father's business takes up time: ' . . . the bearer will tell him that he has not bought one rag since he came to town, he will also tell what trouble his father's business requires. His father need not fear lest he dress like a courtier, since he has no money to go courtier-like . . . ' He will continue his studies on 'the little his father will allow him' and when this runs out come home.

In 1576 he had meanwhile married, an apparently good match to the daughter of Sir William Gerard, Lord Chancellor of Ireland. His father, however, had doubts about it from the start, and he and the Chancellor did not see eye to eye. This caused the young Wynn some worry – 'the jars between his father and Gerard are likely to continue and to light most heavily on the writer' – and he found himself soliciting from his father-in-law funds which his father evidently withheld: 'Reminds him of these matters before his departure for Ireland, that he may remedy the writer's losses and enable him to live in better sort.'

This early correspondence is a foretaste of what was to become, for John Wynn, a lifetime's preoccupation with money and lawsuits. It is strange for someone from such a notably prosperous background that all his life he was beset by money worries.

When Morus died, in August 1580, John his eldest son inherited lands in five North Wales counties. We know a great deal about him and his way of life. We know what he wore, for instance, since a list of his clothes has survived. Because we have these direct insights into the daily life of a great (if perhaps tyrannical) landowner of the period of the British Renaissance we see through him the reality of the life and the time. Part of our information comes, as we shall see, from his own words, since he was an assiduous writer. Much of it comes from the remarkable record contained in the Wynn papers, nearly two centuries of letters (running from 1515 to 1690) which cover in full the period of his lifetime and include letters to and from him and between his contemporaries. Other papers of his have been preserved by Pennant. Here, for instance, he is giving detailed instructions to his chaplain, and in the process letting us see straight into late sixteenth century Gwydir:

FIRST. You shall have the chamber, I shewed you in my gate, private to yourself, with lock, and key, and all necessaries . . .

Before dinner you are to come up and attend grace, or prayers if there be any publicke; and to set up, if there be not greater strangers, above the chyldren – who you are to teach in your own chamber.

When the table, from half downwards, is taken up, then are you to rise, and to walk in the alleys near at hand, until grace time; and to come in then for that purpose.

After dinner, if I be busy, you may go to bowles, shuffel bord, or any other honest decent recreation, until I go abroad . . . If I go to bowles, or shuffel bord, I shall lyke of your company, if the place be not made up with strangers . . .

Avoyd the alehowse, to sytt and keepe drunkards company ther, being the greatest discredit your function can have.

In all his works Wynn writes (even to fellow Welshmen) in clear, robust Elizabethan English; we know, however, that he was a devoted supporter, in the tradition of his family, of his native culture. He received, like his ancestors, the tributes of bards, and employed one, Huw Machno, as household poet. He wrote in Welsh when it suited him. Indeed later in his life he was instrumental in sponsoring the production of a Welsh dictionary.

Nevertheless the fact that he wrote in English, and had of course received his education in England, is to some extent a result of the Acts of incorporation. It had for some time been useful for the upper classes in Wales to know English. Sir John records that his great-grandfather, Maredudd, while still a child in Eifionydd, was sent to school in Caernarfon, 'where he learnt the English tongue, to read, to write, and to understand Latin, a matter of great moment in those days . . . ' Some of

*Ysbyty Ifan, now a small quiet backwater, once a pilgrims' hospice,
was a hotbed of banditry by Sir John's time.*

*The added Wynn chapel faces us in this view of Llanrwst church,
the churchyard of which had run wild, Sir John tells us,
in the troubled times of the late 15th century.*

the books in the old library at Gwydir, which John inherited from his father Morus, were in Welsh, but some were in Latin and in English. The great difference made by the Acts was that it now became not just useful but essential to speak and write English, since English was to be the only language of the law-courts and local government officers in Wales. This fact began a process which increased at speed, the separation of the anglicised gentry, with their London connections and education, from the ordinary people of Wales who still spoke no English and whose culture remained based on their mother tongue. The direct effect of this is that while the Welsh upper classes adopted the English Renaissance, true Welsh culture, after Sir John's time, remained a popular, as opposed to élite, activity. Although Sir John himself straddled the two cultures comfortably, he was probably the last of his kind to do so. When Huw Machno, his court poet, died in 1637, he was not replaced. Sir John was dead himself by then, and Gwydir run by his heir on different principles.

Part of the strain on Sir John's finances was caused by the education of his sons, of which he had in all ten, though several of these died young. In giving them, in full, an English education, he was carrying a step further the habit of his class. It had been normal since the time of Owain Glyndŵr, as we have seen, for the Welsh upper classes to send their heirs for legal training in London, after, presumably, education at home. Now Sir John and his contemporaries sought the benefits of English public schools, and in doing so displayed some adventurousness.

His eldest son, John, went to Bedford Grammar School, followed by Lincoln's Inn. He was joined at the latter by his brother Richard. Owen and Robert went to Westminster, but were moved from there to Eton because of the danger of plague. From there Robert went to St John's College, Cambridge, where the master was a relative, Dr Owen Gwyn, or Wynn. The Welsh influence was strong there, in fact, and another of the college's officials was another relative of the Wynns, John Williams, future Archbishop of York. All this took much organisation and consideration on Sir John's part. It also caused him constant, often distressing, expense.

One glance at the portraits however convinces us that he lived well, and the letters bear this out. A note from his cousin Sir Richard Bulkeley in Beaumaris accompanies 'a hogshead of Graves wine which is very medicinal'. Sir John in fact made his own wine at Gwydir, which, said one grateful recipient, was 'to his thinking more excellent than the grape of France or the wines of Greece or Spain'. At the same time wines were purchased for him in London. His agent 'knows Sir John will drink more sack than claret in Lent because of a fish diet'. His son Owen, who had,

The ruined walls of Tai Penamnen, Maredudd ap Ifan's homestead, may still be seen alongside the old Roman road in Cwm Penamnen.

One of Sir John's Schemes which did not in the end materialise was the reclamation of Traeth Mawr.

after Gray's Inn, acquired connections at court, was able to send him a firkin of the Palermo wine which the King drinks, which he 'had out of the royal cellar from one Edwards, the King's bottleman. Edwards has promised the writer half-a-dozen of the French pears the King eats, as soon as any come to his hands'. Little did James I know the far-reaching results of employing Welsh servants.

Such delicacies enlivened what must have been the standard diet of an agricultural region. Cattle formed the basis of Sir John's day-to-day economy. In 1613, writing to the Privy Council in London, 'excusing himself for not having paid the purchase money for his baronetcy', he goes into some detail about his basic finances. It is July, and a drought in the Conwy valley has burnt up the greater part of the grass and corn; this has affected the sale of cattle (which could not be fattened for the English market) 'which, being his tenants' only means of livelihood, has made them backward in paying their rents.' To a friend he adds that 'the money cannot be paid until the latter part of Michaelmas term, when their drovers return from Kent'. It has been remarked before that the roast beef of old England was in fact Welsh. Cattle by the thousand were reared in Wales and driven to southern England for their final fattening, in the process making the role of the drovers crucial both in economic terms and as a medium of communication. They bore documents and cash, messages and news. Crucially they brought back English money into Wales. Archbishop John Williams, during the Civil War, described them as 'the Spanish fleet which brings hither the little gold and silver we have'.

Sir John did not just have his agents purchase in London exotic wines; he bought, we are surprised to learn, his clothes from there as well. Many of the letters between London and Gwydir mention 'items of apparel'. In 1604 he asked his man to purchase 'a pair of good London boots to keep out the water, this country being so wet', and a roll of taffeta to make a gown for his daughter. In 1611 he asks his son Owen to get him 'a white satin doublet such as Sir John Salusbury wore when he was pictured'.

When, thus, in 1616, an inventory is made of his wardrobe ('a noate of all my clothes') it is not surprising to find that well stocked.

He had two black cloaks and a brown one, lined variously with black velvet and black taffeta; two riding coats, laced with silk and gold lace. He also had two black velvet jackets, and two of cloth laced with gold. He had a satin doublet and breeches, a silk suit, and a black satin suit as well 'that came the same time from London'. He lists various other suits and doublets, and 'one redd quilte waskoote'. Black silk stockings are supported by black silk garters, and a pair of pearl silk stockings is listed,

The old church at Dolwyddelan was built near his home by Maredudd in about 1500.

The small highly-refined brass memorial to Maredudd and his wife is now on a wall in Dolwyddelan church.

along with, presumably for day-to-day wear, three pairs of worsted stockings. He had girdles, and a scarf, and no less than nine black felt hats 'whereof' (slightly puzzlingly) 'fowre bee mens hattes'; with five hatbands to go with them. A rapier and dagger, a riding sword with scarf, all had velvet scabbards. He had some pairs of Spanish leather shoes, two pairs of white boots and one of russet colour. Still on footwear, he boasted three pairs 'of newe blacke boots, and five pare of old blacke boots'. With these went two pairs of damask spurs, and three pairs of gilt spurs.

Sir John was nothing if not up to date, and one of his concerns was to supply his guests at Gwydir with adequate tobacco. The habit of the use of this had arrived in Britain early in the reign of Elizabeth and spread surprisingly fast. It was not a cheap habit, and so may well have been a status symbol among the rising classes, copying the high fashions of the court. 'Tobacco is exceeding dear,' wrote Sir John's London agent in 1604, 'the best 10s. and ounce'. By 1608 it had apparently come down: 'Sends purchases of tobacco at 3s. an oz.'

Keeping up with the London élite from remote North Wales cannot have been easy, and this among other things put a strain on the Wynn finances. One of his weaknesses was for the acquisition of land, including property he could not afford. In 1603 his brother Ellis 'angrily reproaches him for . . . his insatiable passion for purchasing lands with borrowed money'. His failure to clear the debt incurred by the purchase of his baronetcy landed him with the threat of being summoned to appear before the Lord Privy Seal and the Chancellor of the Exchequer. His son and an adviser urge him to pay; but the fact is that (owing to the drought mentioned above) he cannot. None of this stops the flow of 'articles of apparel' and 'the best tobacco', along with wine and delicacies, from London to Gwydir.

Sir John was knighted on 14th May, 1606 and he bought his baronetcy in June 1611. In 1614 he sent his son and heir, also called John, off on a European tour, a rash, and as it turned out tragic decision. Already by the time he reached Marseilles he was short of money, and wrote home to his father asking for funds so that he could go on into Italy. 'I hope you would not that I should be less sufficient than other gent, who seek out ther experience by the same means that I doe.' Evidently the money was forthcoming, since he moved on. In May he crossed by sea to Genoa, and proceeded towards Rome by way of Pisa. By the end of the month he was near Rome. In June and July his father is still writing to him in Florence, and sends £100. The letters are full of local news, of building at Llanrwst and the purchasing of land.

Gwydir, first built by Maredudd, subsequently enlarged by his son, grandson and Sir John, became the main seat of the Wynns.

Some of the stone from the Abbey at Maenan, demolished at the Dissolution of the monasteries, went to the enlargement of Gwydir.

Poignantly, they came back, undelivered. By the time they reached Italy John the younger had died. He fell ill and died in Lucca, on 25th August, 1614.

Sir John did not hear about this at Gwydir until his companions got back, but then he had a full account of his son's regret at the fatal journey, his illness, and his burial at Lucca. Sir John the elder responded by having a memorial designed to be placed on his grave there.

This was of course a cruel blow, since Sir John had schooled his son, as his father had in his case, to take over the estates. He had managed to get him knighted, and in 1606 married to Margaret Cave, daughter of a Northamptonshire knight, whom he hoped (seeing her as future mistress of Gwydir) would, once she had moved to Wales, pick up some Welsh. The marriage was an unhappy one, and when Sir John the younger died he had produced no heirs.

The elder Sir John had been suffering ill-health for some time, and this, and money worries, probably made it worse. As early as 1585 we find him noting, probably for his doctor, 'his symptoms of indisposition'. In 1609 his son-in-law is getting for him a prescription, and herbal and other remedies are prescribed for him in 1610. The complaint is later referred to as 'colic', but some of the recipes, such as one designed to 'draw rheum to the nostrils' suggest that he suffered from catarrh.

If the purpose of John's ill-fated trip to Italy was education and self-improvement, the foreign travels of another son, Maurice, had a more clearly material motive. Maurice went to Hamburg to make money, and in the process advance the family fortunes. This was not a great success either. In 1623 he is complaining to his father that he is worse off than the poorest man's son. In spite of having left home, he apparently expects his father to subsidise his lifestyle. The latter has failed to 'give him the means suitable to a gentleman's son'. At the same time Maurice shows himself perfectly able to get by. He suggests, from Hamburg, buying butter at Chester fair, shipping it via London to Lisbon, 'where butter is very scarce and a market found for it at 9d. a 1b.' At home the continuing corn shortage is troubling his father, and Maurice has written (from Hamburg) to 'a great corn merchant in Newcastle' putting up a project for exchanging corn for Welsh cottons. He has doubts of the success of this, because of distance and the lack of Welsh money. Sir John is expected to finance these and apparently other deals: 'If Sir John does not furnish the writer with money he will be unable to continue his trade'. (As it happened the Newcastle deal fell through because there was a readier market in Northumberland.)

To keep so many sons in so many occupations Sir John had to work hard at home, exploiting to the full the assets of his estates. Rather surprisingly these included the ores of various metals, the quality of which was beginning to arouse interest in the second decade of the seventeenth century. By then the lead mines near Llanrwst were by no means new; it is possible in fact that they were known to the Romans. Of course they belonged to the Gwydir estate. To begin with Sir John let them, but by 1620 he appears to be managing them himself. He writes to Maurice in Hamburg that he intends to send his lead to Bristol, and thence to Spain. The Middlesborough men will buy the rest. (Maurice replies that it was not a wise plan to sell to the Middlesborough men.) By 1620 Sir John has developed a 'foot blast' for smelting the ore, which is pure enough for two tons of it to make a ton of lead. However by 1621 he is complaining that the lead works have been 'a great charge and no gain' and the next year he closed the mines. This brought a plea from Maurice to reopen them and give him a free hand with the results, opining that the ore has been sold too cheaply and that he can find the best market, 'either at Lisbon, Leghorn, Mulligoe, or some other place'. The price of lead, he remarks, like other commodities, is sometimes up, sometimes down. He suggests modernising the mining process by using 'a wimble', an 'instrument used for boring through rocks'. Next year he announces that the price of lead ore has risen. Evidently the mines accordingly reopened, in 1623; Maurice remarks that his father's ore is purer and his mines produce more lead than the northern ones which supply London.

Lead was not the only metal which Sir John's estates possessed. He also set about developing his deposits of copperas (a form of ferrous sulphate) and alum. These were scarce, but unfortunately he found he could not work the latter because someone already had a nation-wide patent on it. Of interest in London also were the mineral waters which occurred in a spring on Sir John's land, doubtless the well-known spa waters at Trefriw. Marble, porphyry, brimstone, and even peat, are the subjects of correspondence between him and potential customers. There was no copper in the Conwy valley, but Sir John had an interest in the mines on Parys Mountain in Anglesey.

We should not forget how extensive his properties were. At one time, in 1625, we find him expressing an interest in the reclamation of land at Tracth Mawr, the delta of the Glaslyn and Dwyryd rivers. Sir Hugh Myddleton had successfully reclaimed 2,000 acres in the Isle of Wight. Sir John wants his help in erecting an embankment across Traeth Mawr. Sir Hugh, from his experience, is not encouraging. He thanks Sir John for his kind letter, but there are snags which would first need to be overcome. It would be necessary to have the consent of the king. They would also need access to 'great stones'. Myddleton says the expense involved would be not hundreds but thousands. He himself is unwilling to get involved, since he is too old and too busy with his own projects; but he 'will endeavour to visit Wynn at a later date'.

The reclamation of Traeth Mawr had to await the arrival of another man of giant ideas. Wynn for his part had enough to do retaining his extensive lands, without embarking on extending them. From the start he was embroiled in disputes, law suits and petitions against other North Wales landowners, notably William Williams of Cochwillan and Thomas Price of Plas Iolyn. The matter concerned leases and occupation of land, and Williams sought to cast doubt on Wynn's rights by faulting the legitimacy of his line: his great-grandfather had been married to the illegitimate daughter of the house of Cochwillan. It was a sore point, and perhaps the motivation for the book in which Wynn set out the grandeur of his inheritance. There is a tradition that he physically attacked William Williams in Conwy church, perhaps the event referred to in a letter of December 1592, for which he was fined £100. 'If John Wynn of Gwydir will submit to the censure of the Court of the Marches, his fine of £100 may be reduced to £50. The offence was but a blow and the occasion great.' The wrangle with Thomas Price ended up in the court of Star Chamber. Price's contention was again ancestral: Wynn falsely claimed descent from a prince of Wales. He added more specific faults, referring to a 'riot' at Llanrwst and the committing of someone's mother to the stocks 'because her son would not sell his lands to Wynn'. The whole business smacks rather of personal animosity, and Wynn seems, if not outright quarrelsome, at least to have been capable of making enemies. He managed to quarrel also with his eminent kinsman, John Williams, Lord Keeper and future Archbishop of York (at that time Bishop of St Asaph). Indeed, as he says in his own words, he was (at least at one time) much subject to choler. He had in fact consciously set about controlling this. Possibly the outbreaks of temper were connected to his occasional indisposition.

That particular passage of self-revelation occurs in his 'History of the Gwydir Family' and shows us a thoughtful, duly humble man. He had at one time fallen out with his uncle and neighbour Owen, who had to carry his hay across the valley from Trefriw to near Llanrwst, and hence across Sir John's land. This issue, as trivial matters often do, caused disproportionate tension, until it seemed in fact as if someone might get killed. Another relative being present when uncle and nephew were disputing warned Sir John that more was to be gained by tolerance than 'headiness and rashness', 'which counsel of his took deep root in me and

The lead mines at Trefriw, in operation until modern times, formed a part of Sir John's estate and one of his sources of income.

ever after, and to my great good bridled my choler whereunto I was much subject.'

Sir John in fact reveals himself to us more fully in his books than his letters, as garrulous, conscientious and opinionated. It seems likely that the 'History' had a particular motive: the establishment for all time of the eminence and pedigree of his family, an integrity which the Star Chamber case brought by his neighbours had attempted to take from him. He warns his son to expect hostility arising from envy. He says in his book that ever since the time of Rhodri Fawr there had been an eminent member of his family, sometimes many at the same time. Whereas poverty soon forgets whence it be descended, 'a great temporal blessing it is, and a great heart's ease to a man to find that he is well descended', a comfort unknown to 'upstarts and gentlemen of the first head' who then, he says, come to hate true gentlemen 'for no other cause but that they were gentlemen'.

In spite of such clarity of purpose Sir John shows himself again and again unable to resist indulging in a good yarn. Hence we have, along with a great many strings of geneology, a good few insights into the rough-and-tumble of earlier times. 'You are to understand that in those days in that wild world every man stood upon his guard and went not abroad but in sort and so armed as if he went to the field to encounter with his enemies.' Sir John's view of his ancestors' Wales, in which murder and feud were (at least in his perception) a way of life, makes us aware that by his own day the world was comparatively settled. Quarrelsomeness certainly seems to have been a characteristic common to both times, but it is notable that his contemporaries took him to court, when their forebears would have tried to get him assassinated.

The book, having ranged backwards and forwards between ancient history and contemporary anecdote, ends abruptly, clearly abandoned unfinished, at the point when Maredudd his great-grandfather had brought under control the robbers of Ysbyty Ifan. It is supplemented by some 'Memoirs', which are notes on local history from the point of view of the leading families of the area, including his own. Here we have, among much else of interest, some details of the life of his uncle, Robert Wynn, who built Plas Mawr in Conwy. He had been wounded at the siege of Boulogne while serving in the household of Sir Philip Holby. He and his master served the king in his campaigns in Scotland, and went as ambassador to the Emperor Charles V. When Mary Tudor succeeded, and the state religion turned back to Catholicism, Sir Philip lost favour 'by reason of his religion' and was dismissed, whereon Robert Wynn came back to North Wales and built his great house in Conwy.

*Sir John refers to the gatehouse at Gwydir, which still forms
a prominent aspect of the homestead.*

*Among many raw materials Sir John exported mineral water,
probably from the ancient wells at Trefriw.*

In keeping with the attitudes of his time, the British Renaissance, Wynn had an interest in science as well as antiquity. Even in his histories the emphasis is on close objective observation. He had in his library a copy of Camden's 'Britannia', of 1586, and Dr David Powell's 'Historie of Cambria', of 1584, both representative of the inquiring approach of the new age, as well as more traditional works such as Geoffrey of Monmouth, and the Welsh Triads. As a serious historian he also used first-hand accounts of the past, such as Giraldus Cambrensis, and Matthew Paris' 'Chronica Maiora'. There is no doubt, both from his reading and his desire for the memorial of his writing, from his employment of a court bard and his patronage of the 1604 Welsh dictionary, that he took literature seriously.

An interesting example of Sir John's approach to history is his 'Ancient Survey of Penmaenmawr', in which an eclectic compilation of local folklore and tradition is combined with painstaking field work evidently carried out by himself. He opts very firmly for the historical veracity of the Llys Helig legend: the story that the bay between Penmaenmawr and the Orme was once dry land. He points out that the stumps of trees may be seen below sea level, as indeed they still may. ' . . . this I speake as an eye witness, havynge seene the rootes my sealf and taken them upp, soe that ytt shoulde seeme that this vale before the inundacion was a woodland country.'

From all this it may be seen that Sir John was busy. He had at the same time his public duties. In keeping with the tradition of his family and the custom of great landowners, he held various official posts. He was a member of the Council of the Marches, Deputy Lieutenant for Caernarfonshire and twice Sheriff. One of the great disappointments of his life, however, was his failure to get elected as knight for the shire of Caernarfon, the equivalent of M.P., in 1620. Although his assistants gathered what support they could, and although Sir John seems to have been willing to bribe the Sheriff, rival families (their 'enemies') ganged up against them.

Beyond a few necessary trips to London Sir John did not travel much, and most of his life was spent at Gwydir. It is known that the Earl of Leicester, who had rights and property in North Wales and thus was acting as Wynn's overlord, summoned him to service in the Low Countries; and since there is a gap in the correspondence then Wynn may well have gone – but it somehow seems unlikely that if he had done we would hear no more about it. The movements of his sons are fully chronicled. Indeed their wide-ranging careers improved on his own in terms of distinction. Two of them were knighted during his lifetime,

*Plas Mawr in Conwy was built by Sir John's
distinguished uncle, Robert Wynn.*

which no doubt gave him paternal satisfaction. One, Richard, had entered the Lord Chamberlain's department, and became secretary to Prince Charles. In that capacity he went with the prince to Spain, in 1623, to woo the Infanta. He went with extreme reluctance, since it was 'a dangerous and expensive journey', and he did not think much of Spain when he got there. 'Castile and Aragon together are not worth one of the worst counties in Wales. The Welsh mountains are but mole-hills, but their barrenness is most fruitful in comparison with Spain. Henceforth the writer will believe everything reported of another country rather than go and see it.'

It is significant that this enforced trip hit the Wynn finances, and we find Sir John bemoaning this to his relative John Williams, then Lord Keeper. His son's debts will be increased by the journey, and he himself, he says, is £3000 in debt. His rates and revenues have fallen this year by more than £400 because of agricultural failure in the uplands. This is the same period that he and his son Maurice, in Hamburg, are corresponding about his minerals.

Sir Richard continued his royal connections after the death of his father, becoming Groom of the Bedchamber and Treasurer of the Household of Queen Henrietta Maria in the reign of Charles I.

Among the business which occupied Sir John's considerable energy, at home, was the improvement of his house, which he set about early, in the 1590's. He added a half-timbered section, and in 1597 he reminds himself in a note to 'finish the gate-house chamber'. He also restyled the garden and surrounding area. It was in his library or study, 'the old paper room', that the letters and memoranda which give us so much information about Sir John were collected, remaining there until the late eighteenth century, after which they were dispersed in three major groups. We are fortunate that work in the 1920's by the National Library of Wales collected and catalogued the dispersed contents of Sir John's study to give us now such a clear view of himself, his heirs and descendants.

He left them his lands in good shape, and the family continued to prosper. His daughter Mary had married, in August 1596, Sir Roger Mostyn, ensuring a dominant position in North Wales for their descendants by the combining of the two great landowning families. Both the Mostyns and the Wynns continue, to the present day, to own much land and carry much weight in the region. Sir John Wynn's line itself died out, however, when the fourth baronet died in 1674 with no male issue, and his only child (also Mary) subsequently married Robert Bertie, who became the first Duke of Ancaster. Gwydir and the estates then descended through his family with ramifications which need not concern us.

That Sir John was a great man is an impression we gain partly from his own view of his position, partly from the attitude of those around him. It is not so clear that he was a happy one, and occasionally, in his asides, there are hints that he was not. Wielding such power (perhaps he felt) should have been easier than it turned out to be. Bothered by ill-health and debt, he was also conscious of being surrounded by enemies. 'You must learne to know yo'r frendes from yo'r enemyes,' he advises his eldest son. 'As I shall leave you frendes so also enymyes whose cheife motive ys that I prosper.'

A Changing World

In the course of a bit more than a thousand years we have seen the order of things in Britain change a number of times, dynasties and populations, languages and even religions. The face of the country itself has changed, becoming barer under the pressure of land use and the increasingly commercial attention paid to it by its great owners. From the early clearances of the Dark Ages in the time of Maelgwn, a process of bringing land into more intensive use gradually accelerated towards the mass enclosures of the 18th and 19th centuries. A process of taming took place too in the social world, a gradually increasing complexity of administration replacing monocratic rule and law taking over from violence as the prime enforcing agency.

Yet in a way nothing had changed. North Wales was ruled still by an old aristocracy of continuous, indigenous lineage. Though often divided by mutual competition, they maintained their dominance by superior wit as well as wealth, the most ambitious and determined of them coming out on top. They owned the land. They always had. They regarded it as their right.

Politically these men throughout normally maintained an alliance based on common interest with the neighbouring country, whether it be Powys or England. If they exercised their power discreetly they were left in peace. The common people normally found it expedient to go along with this, since they enjoyed their minimal rights only by acquiescence to the status quo. Yet their tolerance could not be taken for granted, nor could it be stretched, and hence it provided a limiting curb on what might otherwise have been the exercise of autocratic power. Towards the end of our period it is becoming obvious that the great landowners, who were also the officers of administration, knew that the best interests of their tenants were also their own. If they were to prosper, so must those who provided their wealth. Pushed too far by exploitation they would rebel. Yet this had always been the case, as history had shown. In the meantime the generality, in the sixteenth century as in the sixth, lived in a simple agricultural world, in which they were able, and content, to maintain the long traditions of their ancestors.

All this was just about to change. A new world was coming into being, based first on international trade and then on industry. We have seen the start of this in the entrepreneurial activities of the Wynns. It was now about to undergo a quantum leap.

Sir John Wynn stands at a pivotal point in this programme. That is why he is of such interest to this story, and also why I have decided to break it at this point. It is tempting in fact to make him not only the last figure in the first half but the first in the second. In many ways he was the apotheosis of the old regime; yet through him we have seen the coming into being of the new. World prices of lead, for instance, affected his economies. Though Madocks is credited traditionally with introducing industry to North Wales, it was Sir John who in fact brought in the first elements of industrial technology, when he developed a 'foot blast', in 1620, for smelting ore, and if indeed he followed his son's advice to introduce a 'wimble', a machine for boring through rocks. He toyed with thoughts of civil engineering. In his time legalistic constitutional rights became an effective curb to the sheer wielding of power; and people took him to court in a way that would have been unthinkable to his princely ancestors. His power was curtailed in at least two other ways. He was accountable to courts outside his own control; and he was dependent on his subordinates, rather than they on him.

The figures in the landscape of the second volume of this book will move in a different world. None of them originated in the immediate area on which they stamped their mark, and at least some too left greater marks on a broader plain. The world for them has opened up, in a way foreshadowed by Maurice Wynn at Hamburg or Richard Wynn at court. It is a world in which money and influence flows through North Wales with the increase in travel and mobility which the eighteenth century brought and the nineteenth century developed.

We shall see, among other things, how Madocks was instrumental in turning North Wales into an exporting country; how in their different spheres both the first Marquess of Anglesey and David Lloyd George raised the status of North Wales to a place on the world stage; and how great talent and great personality could flower in North Wales' unrestricting ambience in the form of such an idiosyncratic hero as Sir Clough Williams-Ellis.

We shall see, in fact, in the end, how North Wales and the giants who have walked in its landscape have each contributed to and been affected by the other.

Bibliography

Chapter 1
N.J. Higham; *The English Conquest – Gildas and Britain in the fifth century* (Manchester University Press).
Michael Winterbottom (ed.), *Gildas: The Ruin of Britain and other works* (Pphillimore).
Lady Charlotte Guest (ed. and trans.), *The Mabinogion* (Everyman).
Patrick K. Ford, (ed. and trans.), *The Mabinogion* (University of California Press).
Robert Graves, *The White Goddess* (Faber).
John Davies, *A History of Wales* (Penguin).
W. Bezant Lowe, *The Heart of Northern Wales*.
Thomas Firbank, *A Country of Memorable Honour* (Harrap).

Chapter 2
Giraldus, *The Itinerary Through Wales* (Everyman).
David Stephenson, *The Governance of Gwynedd* (University of Wales Press).
Sir John Lloyd, *A History of Wales*.
John Davies, *A History of Wales* (Penguin).
Richard Avent, *Castles of the Princes of Gwynedd* (HMSO).

Chapter 3
R.R. Davies, *The Revolt of Owain Glyndŵr* (Oxford).
Sir John Lloyd, *Owen Glendower* (Oxford).
John Davies, *A History of Wales* (Penguin).
Thomas Pennant, *Tours in Wales*.
Douglas Hague and Cynthia Warhurst, *Excavations at Sycharth Castle, Denbighshire* (Archeologia Cambrensis).
Gwyn Williams, *Introduction to Welsh Poetry* (Faber).
Anthony Conran (ed.), *The Penguin Book of Welsh Verse* (Penguin).
E.F. Jacob, *The Fifteenth Century* (Oxford English History).

Chapter 4
J. Gwynfor Jones, *The Wynn Family of Gwydir*.
J. Gwynfor Jones (ed.), *History of the Gwydir Family* by Sir John Wynn (Gomer Press).
Calendar of the Wynn Papers (University of Wales Press).
Thomas Pennant, *Tours in Wales*.
W. Bezant Lowe (ed.), *An Ancient Survey of Penmaenmawr* by Sir John Wynn.
John Davies, *A History of Wales* (Penguin).

Acknowledgement

The author would like to thank Mr Peter Welford for providing him with information and insights on the subject of Sir John Wynn.